gardening & planting by the mon

by the

2018

gardening & planting by the moon

2018

nick kollerstrom

quantum

LONDON • NEW YORK • TORONTO • SYDNEY

quantum

An imprint of Foulsham Publishing Ltd

The Old Barrel Store, Drayman's Lane, Marlow, Bucks SL7 2FF

Foulsham books can be found in all good bookshops and direct from www.foulsham.com

Dedicated to the memory of Frau Maria Thun, pioneer of lunar gardening

ISBN: 978-0-572-04694-1

Cover photograph © Garden Picture Library

Series, format and layout design © 2017 Foulsham Publishing Ltd

The moral right of the author has been asserted

A CIP record for this book is available from the British Library

Typeset in India by Lapiz Digital Services, Chennai

Printed and bound by CPI Group (UK) Ltd, Croydon, CR0 4YY

Contents

The pull of the Moon is considerable. Not only does it move tides twice a day, it pulls on the Earth. Many gardeners and farmers are rediscovering the benefit of planting according to its phases, part of a profound knowledge neglected by modern techniques.

Harmony, A New Way of Looking at our World, by HRH The Prince of Wales, with Tony Juniper and Ian Skelly, 2010, p.137.

Introduction	6
Perspectives	8
Cycles of the Sky	14
Using the Star Zodiac	19
The Rhythm of the Sun	23
The Moon and Crop Yield	27
The Moon and Fertility	34
Gardening Aspects	40
The Organic Way	44
Monthly Tasks in the Vegetable Garden	47
How to Use the Lunar Calendar	56
The Lunar Calendar	64
The Seasons of 2018	139
Further Reading	142
Index	143

Introduction

To everything there is a season and a time to every purpose under heaven: a time to be born and a time to die: a time to plant, and a time to pluck up what is planted ...

Ecclesiastes 3:1–2

very gardener and farmer wants the best possible crops, and we all try out various ways of achieving that end. Since you are reading this, you must have wondered whether you could get better results if you planted in harmony with the cycles of the Moon – I believe you can.

For as long as anyone can remember, people have held a belief in the efficacy of such a practice, and various different traditions have developed. In many countries today, lunar calendars are available for farmers and gardeners, and there is considerable evidence to show that crops can benefit from the correct use of a lunar gardening guide. It is our hope that this manual will come to be used not only for its practical advantages, but also as an inspiration to gardeners to become more aware of the life-rhythms in nature, which mysteriously connect the growth of plants with cosmic time-cycles.

The aim of the book is not only to provide detailed planting and gardening advice, but also to stimulate interest in, and research into, the question of lunar influence, within the context of the burgeoning organic movement. Those who simply wish to apply the recommended gardening advice for 2017 can turn straight to the calendar pages.

The range of lunar gardening guides available often offer conflicting advice. This is because old traditions have become confused over time and the rise of the bio-dynamic movement, founded in 1924 by the Austrian teacher and philosopher Rudolf Steiner (1861–1925) has gained a great following. The recommendations here may not be the same as those in other lunar gardening guides, but they may have a better chance of producing dependable crop improvements.

Gardeners work with time. They continually make judgements on how the seasons are progressing, what the weather may do, and so on, always in the context of having limited time available. Gardening and farming, however, can take on an extra dimension if one is aware that, besides these practical considerations, there are also basic cycles of the heavens to which animals and the plant world are attuned. Plants receive their energy for growth from the Sun but, in other more subtle ways, they are continually affected by the Moon's ever-changing rhythms. A decision as to when to plant a tree should take such lunar cycles into account, just as a sailor puts to sea only when the tides are right.

During the twentieth century, systematic experiments began to determine how the various lunar cycles played a part in plant metabolism, growth and development. Certain keys to understanding the relationship of plant responses to lunar influence have now emerged and can be incorporated into a gardener's or farmer's plans as to when best to carry out various tasks, in particular sowing, planting and harvesting. I wish to express deep gratitude towards Simon Best: he and I composed *Planting by the Moon* in 1980, and worked with it through the 1980s, as a synthesis of time-honoured traditions and twentieth-century research. Its basic ideas are here slightly developed.

There is also mounting evidence that the lunar cycle, particularly the Full Moon and the lunar nodes, has a considerable effect on horse breeding. This is explained in more detail on pages 37–38 and I hope in further years to integrate this information into the calendar.

The Moon affects us as well as plants and animals, though not so directly and not, I believe, so powerfully. A paper (Professor Cajochen, *Current Biology*, July 2013) on human sleep patterns during the lunar month concludes that we sleep better at the New Moon; brain-wave activity indicating deep sleep was 30% less at the Full Moon, and the time taken to fall asleep was longer. This theory relates to the idea promoted in this calendar of encouraging festivals and celebration at the Full Moon, while the New Moon is a better time for new beginnings.

Various astrological and related concepts are used in the calendar, but readers unfamiliar with such things need not worry: this book provides clear, step-by-step explanations, highlighting both the continuous rhythms of energy that ebb and flow and should resonate with the sympathetic worker, and also the specific moments, or celestial events, which the gardener should endeavour to catch.

Those who use ephemerides or astrology programs may notice that the Moon sign entries in our diary differ from those they will find there. This is because astrological programs use the tropical zodiac, whereas ours use the sidereal calendar, indicating where the star constellations are, and the systems differ by two days of the Moon's motions. This is explained on page 15.

This calendar also gives dates for the 'Moons of celebration', the sacred Moons of the Muslim, Jewish, Hindu and Chinese New Years, and the Full Moon of May, which the Buddhists celebrate a month after the Full Moon that fixes Easter. It also includes the 12 lunar months of the Muslim year.

To extend the usefulness of the calendar to new buyers, it also includes a full 15 months of diary pages.

If you want to look at some of the evidence in support of the recommendations given here, there is a website collecting experimental results: www.considera.org. It is encouraging that someone is collecting the raw data of these experiments and let's hope that continues. Plants are so sensitive to these subtle influences, as science is just beginning to discover. Also, a couple of my published articles on the subject are on the UK Biodynamic website at: www.biodynamic.org.uk/ Research.htm#Mares%20fertility. One of these shows how very much horses respond to the lunar month – as, one assumes, do all living creatures. You will find an index of all Nick Kollerstrom's research, including planting by the moon, at www.astrozero.co.uk/astroscience/koll2indx.htm

Perspectives

Pleiades rising in the dawning sky,
  Harvest is nigh.
Pleiades setting in the waning night,
  Ploughing is right.
Forty days and nights in the turning year
  They disappear.
When they shine again in the morning shade,
  Sharpen your blade.

Hesiod, *Works and Days,* eighth century BC

 lants are adapted to the primary cycles of time – the day, month and year. This book focuses on the second of these, the monthly rhythms that are so important for the plant world. These monthly cycles are lunar, in contrast with the day and year, which are solar. It may be a mystery as to how plants respond to these monthly cycles, but that doesn't stop them from being of practical value in the garden and on the farm.

The sensitivity of plants to minute levels of energy was first systematically studied by the Indian scientist Sir Jagadis Chandra Bose (1858–1937) in the early years of the twentieth century. Using carefully designed apparatus, he produced a mass of evidence showing that plants have a far greater capacity to respond to subtle environmental stimuli than had previously been believed.

Plants, small animals and birds are attuned to the natural electric and magnetic fields of the Earth. By altering such fields in the laboratory, scientists have been able to alter the rate and other characteristics of a plant's growth as well as the direction in which a bird will fly. The Earth's geomagnetic field has been shown to vary with the lunar month and to bring about some large-scale effects.

The Biosphere

One of the first lunar-cycle effects to be clearly demonstrated was in rainfall. This was reported in 1962 by two independent groups of researchers, one in the northern and one in the southern hemisphere. Their results appeared in *Science* magazine – in the same issue, for mutual support! The rhythm of the Moon's pull on the sea causes tides to reach their highest twice a month, on average a day after the Full and New Moons. Average rainfall also follows this twice-monthly rhythm, peaking three or four days after the Full and New Moons. The two groups of researchers examined 50 years of data and found that the magnitude of the lunar effect they had discovered varied with the level of solar activity.

The Earth's magnetic field is a membrane that shields us from solar radiation. We know that it pulsates to a monthly rhythm, strengthening following the Full Moon. The geomagnetic field stays low for the week before the Full Moon, then it increases sharply, remaining high for some days.

Thunderstorms recorded by Eastern US weather stations over the years 1942–65 followed a pattern similar to that seen in the geomagnetism data. They decreased for a few days before the Full Moon, and then increased sharply, peaking two days after the Full Moon. Conversely, there was a definite decrease on days following the New Moon. In contrast, a survey of hurricanes and typhoons in the North Atlantic, from 80 years of data, found they tended to occur 20 per cent more frequently on days following both the Full and New Moons.

So, the biosphere as a whole responds to this fundamental cycle. The effect of this pulsation upon climate is slowly becoming recognised as science, not just folklore. The changing Sun–Moon angle causes huge electric and magnetic changes in the upper atmosphere. It is therefore little more than common sense to affirm that both gardeners and farmers should take notice of it.

Traditional Lore

There is a wide but fragmentary body of folk-knowledge, gleaned from many cultures and various ages, that reflects the age-old belief of farmers and gardeners that the Moon somehow influences the growth of their crops.

Hesiod, the Greek astronomer and contemporary of Homer, is considered to have written the first lunar agricultural manual, in the eighth century. His poem *Works and Days* advised farmers on how to regulate many activities by the phases of the Moon. Later, this emphasis on the lunar phases became particularly important to Roman farmers. Lunar-planting rules were recorded by Cato and Pliny. The primary rules, many of which have persisted in folklore to this day, focus on the differences between the effects of the waxing and waning Moon.

This same view was current in seventeenth-century England: *'he* [the farmer] *shall gather and carry into his house whatsoever he would have to endure and last long, at such times as the Moone shall decrease'* (La Maison Rustique, 1616).

Basically, whatever required growth was started during the waxing phase, and whatever needed to dry, cure or decrease without decay was dealt with in the waning phase. The dark time just before the New Moon was said to be especially favourable for the latter activities. Thus, planting crops, picking grapes for wine and shearing sheep were carried out during the waxing Moon, and general harvesting of crops, felling timber and castration of animals during the waning phase.

Pliny was a keen observer of nature, shown by his multi-volume *History of Nature*. He believed he could discern how, *'that tiny creature the ant, at the Moon's conjunction keeps quite quiet, but at full Moon works busily even in the nights.'* If there was a problem with the ground being damp, then Pliny's advice was to sow seeds in the waning half of the lunar cycle so that the land could dry out. Seventeenth-century British gardening guides quoted Pliny on this subject.

The various facets of lunar lore were transmitted, both verbally and in scattered writings, down through the ages and across cultures to the present day, although modern collections of these adages markedly illustrate the confusion of ideas in this area. Grafting and planting-out operations should be performed during the waxing Moon because rising sap is said to help the formation of new shoots or the establishment of a new graft. Lawns are said to benefit from being sown during the waxing phase, a time also propitious for transplanting trees and flowers. One of the oldest maxims that recommended using the waxing/waning division with respect to planting is as follows: crops which produce their yield above ground should be planted during the waxing Moon, whereas those that produce below ground should be sown during the waning Moon. This idea can be found in many parts of the world, but so can similar ideas which modify or contradict it.

In particular, it is claimed that sowing around the Full or New Moon will improve crop growth. Here again opinions vary; for example, some advocate planting in the days immediately preceding the New Moon so that seeds will have germinated and be ready to grow as the Moon begins to increase. More widespread is the opposite opinion, that crops should be sown just before the Full Moon. This is the view particularly associated with the work of Lili Kolisko, who came to Britain from Germany in 1936. The results of her years of study were published in 1938–9, and claimed that seed germination, and especially the unfolding of the first leaves of young shoots, pointed to the days prior to Full Moon as an optimal sowing time, and those prior to New Moon as the worst, in terms of speed of growth.

However, although Moon phase does affect plant metabolism, there is little reliable evidence that sowing at any particular point in the lunar-phase cycle will influence the final yield. Seedling germination and growth may increase around and especially just before the Full Moon, but such effects may not show up in the final crop yield. Much of the confusion of traditional belief may have arisen from such a confounding of different aspects of plant growth.

More recently, it used to be a common custom in the west of England to gather in the 'hoard fruit' in the 'shrinking of the Moon'. Apples bruised in the harvesting would then tend to preserve better over the winter. This accords with modern studies showing varying plant water-absorption at the different phases, suggesting that some facets of lunar lore may be vindicated by modern research.

The Four Elements

Although modern lunar gardening guides tend to disagree on many issues, they do concur on one point: they all use a notion of dividing the zodiac into four periods, each connected with a particular element – Earth, Air, Fire and Water.

At the core of this calendar is a four-element pattern, generated by the motion of the Moon against the stars, a modern system, based on an ancient idea, that has been in use for several decades and is now proving its usefulness and accuracy.

Each month, the Moon moves around the sky against the 12 constellations of the zodiac, each of which has its particular affinity with one of the four elements.

Each of the elements has three constellations linked to it, and these are spaced equally around the circle of the zodiac. The diagram below shows the sky-triangles, or trigons, that map the three related signs. The 27-day orbit of the Moon against the stars means that each element lasts for two or three days and is repeated every nine days. The elements of Earth, Water, Air and Fire are said to influence the growth and performance of a particular sort of plant, respectively Root, Leaf, Flower and Fruit-seed. Further division into the well-known 12 signs of the zodiac is secondary in this scheme.

The four-element theory was first expressed by Empedocles in the fifth century BC in Sicily. He believed that nature used the four elements – fire, wind, sea and stone – to paint with, just as an artist uses four colours. The ancient Greeks also applied the four-element theory in their four temperaments, much used in their medical practice, defining people's characters by their related element.

There are further parallels in other areas of knowledge. Physicists work with 12 types of 'fundamental' particles and four states of matter – solid, liquid, gas and plasma (hot, and above the atmosphere). Biochemists describe four types of code in the DNA strand, while Jungian psychology talks of four temperaments.

The four-element cycle underlying the zodiac

The theory is that in nature there are four kinds of subtle energy, 'formative forces', which work to influence the way a plant will develop, linking the time of sowing to the final condition of the crop when harvested. These forces are activated by the Moon's passage through the zodiac-elements, as the seed is sown. This pattern of influence is to do with the pattern of the stars rather than the zodiac used in modern astrology.

The Star Rhythm

The sequence of element days, the star rhythm, runs: Root days, Flower days, Leaf days and then Fruit-seed days.

Root days are the times to sow carrots, potatoes, radishes and other root crops. These days occur when the Moon passes in front of the stars of one of three planets linked to the Earth element: Taurus, Virgo and Capricorn. When this happens, the

Moon is said to have an Earth-type energy. If the weather is unsuitable for sowing those particular crops, simply wait for the next set of Root days nine days later.

Root days relate to the Earth signs *Taurus* *Virgo* *Capricorn*

Leaf days are times when the Moon is in front of the constellations related to Water – Cancer, Scorpio and Pisces – and is the time to sow lettuce, cabbage and other leafy crops.

Leaf days relate to the Water signs *Cancer* *Scorpio* *Pisces*

Flower days relate to the Air signs – Gemini, Libra and Aquarius – and are the best times to sow broccoli, globe artichoke, cauliflowers and similar plants.

Flower days relate to the Air signs *Gemini* *Libra* *Aquarius*

Fruit-seed days relate to the Fire signs – Aries, Leo and Sagittarius – and are ideal for sowing tomatoes, beans and peas.

Fruit-seed days relate to the Fire signs *Aries* *Leo* *Sagittarius*

One can visualise this as a sequence of plant development. First the root descends into the soil (Earth), then the leaves unfold, with water flowing up the stem and transpiring out through the leaves (Water). Then come the flowers, emitting their fragrance to attract bees and butterflies to fertilise them (Air). Lastly, the flowers fall away as the heat of the summer shrivels up the plant, drying it into the final stage of the seed (Fire). The tiny seeds contain the essence of the flower, just as fire is the least material or least dense of the four elements. Biologically, one may prefer to view the last stage as Warmth rather than Fire, emphasising its constructive role in a process of maturation.

This element cycle, linked to the stars and therefore known as a sidereal rhythm (from the Latin word for star, *sidera*), is one of the two fundamental lunar cycles relevant for a lunar-gardening calendar. The other is the better-known waxing-waning lunar month of 29.5 days, which influences fertility, germination, water absorption and metabolism. The chapter covering the Moon and crop yield (see page 27) looks at the evidence for this element cycle affecting living things, and why a modern grower should take notice of it. It appears especially relevant to organic growers who wish to work in harmony with the living rhythms of the Earth, as it seems to require a 'living' soil for the element rhythm to work; whereas, lunar-phase effects will turn up anywhere!

Belief in the Moon's influence on the fertility of plants was once firmly embedded in the consciousness of ancient people and, as this is rediscovered scientifically today, farmers are again coming to regard the application of lunar cycles as a valuable practice.

Frau Maria Thun

This year, I would once again like to dedicate this lunar gardening guide to Maria Thun (1922–2012) the great modern pioneer of the subject. Her calendar, translated into over twenty languages, sold maybe two hundred thousand copies globally each year, with no advertising. Her books show her creative investigation of the subject, and how she tested better ways for organic growers. In my opinion, her calendar really worked, which is why she will be remembered. Maria discovered the basic four-element rhythm: Empedocles discovered the four elements, Vettius Valens put them into the Zodiac, and in 1953 Maria Thun discovered plant response to them. This four-element rhythm is now used in all bio-dynamic calendars.

I went to visit her farm in the 1990s in Darmstadt and saw her marvellous experiments. Many of the villagers assisted her. One experiment that impressed me involved milking a group of rams every morning for sixty days. She measured the milk, then every day she made butter from the milk and weighed it – a wonderfully simple experiment! The best time in terms of the Moon-trigons was the fire element, what we here call the Fruit-seed days. My new book *Farmer's Moon* contains further details; as this is gardening guide, it only gives a brief synopsis.

Her last publication was surely her most successful – *When Wine Tastes Best*. Again (and it may not surprise you) the fire-trigon turns out to be the best time for opening that special bottle of wine; the experience of tasting is said to be best when the Moon is in a fire-element sign! Thun didn't claim to have invented this notion, but rather affirmed that British wine-tasters had somehow discovered it. I went to one of the wine-connoisseur shops (in Maida Vale, London) which was advocating this new theory, to see delighted wine-tasters admiring the bouquet on an air-day (that's a flower-day in this calendar). Large-scale wine fairs have been using this elemental theory for a few years now, which I suggest indicates that Thun's four-element model is catching on.

A group of fellow lunar-gardening calendar composers and myself have recently formed a guild, somewhat in the wake of Thun's passing, to help optimise our skills in writing the calendars. The guild comprises Sherry Wildfeuer, American writer of the Stella Natura bio-dynamic calendar; Brian Keats of the Antipodean Astro Calendar and Mark Moodie, bio-dynamics researcher who lives in Stroud. I met Brian a couple of years ago when we were setting up this guild, and he had just been to Norway to see the Aurora Borealis, because his calendar predicted that it would be a good time to see them! He explained to us about the fairly new concept of supermoons and how they work – I've put them in this year's calendar. Brian Keats publishes monthly weather guides for the year ahead – now that takes courage! Each calendar has a different angle. Our calendar tries to be as solidly based as possible upon the available evidence, and also tries to integrate the new, bio-dynamic perspective with British Renaissance lunar-gardening traditions.

Cycles of the Sky

Time faire, to sowe or to gather be bold,
but set or remove when the weather is cold.
Cut all thing or gather, the Moone in the wane,
but sowe in encreasing, or give it his bane.

Thomas Tusser, *Five Hundred Points of Good Husbandry,* 1573

s we look at the stars scattered across the night sky and the ever-changing face of the Moon, we cannot but be struck by a sense of the primal mystery of the cosmos and wonder if we are linked to it in some fundamental way.

The Moon has four basic monthly cycles, and these describe its motion in relation to the Sun (synodic), to the stars (sidereal), to the Earth (apogee–perigee) and to the ecliptic plane (nodal).

The Synodic or Phase Cycle — Moon and Sun

As the Moon waxes and wanes each month, it mirrors the Sun's light from different angles and appears to increase and decrease in size. It takes 29.5 days to do this. When Full, the Moon is opposite to the Sun in the sky, so that as it rises, the Sun sets. The four positions of the Full, New and quarter Moons each month are shown in the calendar. There are usually 12 Full Moons in a year.

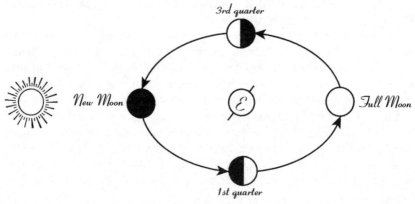

The synodic or phase cycle

The Sun and Moon meet together in the sky at New Moon, when it becomes impossible to see the Moon for several days because it is so close to the Sun. The Greek word *synodos* means 'meeting' and also signified copulation, pointing to the deep connection this cycle has to germination and fertility.

The Sidereal Cycle – Moon and Stars

Once in 27.3 days, the Moon orbits the Earth against the fixed stars. In this time, called a sidereal month, the Moon returns to the same part of the heavens as seen from Earth. It also revolves on its own axis in this same period so that its 'face' is always directed towards the Earth.

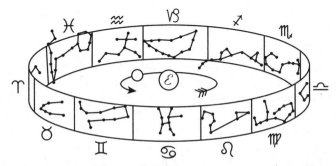

The sidereal cycle

The Moon moves against the same background of constellations as the other planets. It orbits around the Earth in a plane similar to that in which the Earth and planets orbit around the Sun (called the ecliptic). The constellations against which the Moon and planets are seen to move are therefore of special importance. Since ancient times they have been regarded as divided into the 12 constellations of the zodiac. The Moon therefore spends two to three days in each zodiacal constellation. This cycle has a special link with the four elements, as these are related to the signs of the zodiac.

The Apogee–Perigee Cycle – Moon and Earth

The Moon moves around the Earth in an elliptical orbit, so its distance from the Earth varies considerably through the month. Every 27.2 days it reaches its apogee, furthest away from the Earth, then draws closest at its perigee, when it appears larger in the sky, pulls on the tides more strongly, and appears to move faster against the stars. This means that the time that the Moon spends in each of the 12 zodiacal divisions varies by more than 30 per cent in a single rotation. At perigee,

15

the Moon is moving fastest against the stars, and it takes only two days to pass through one zodiacal division, whereas at apogee, when moving slowest, it takes almost three days.

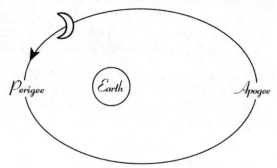

The apogee–perigee cycle

This cycle cannot be seen in the sky, as the apparent change in the size of the Moon is too small to notice. Its effect can be seen in the calendar, however, as the Moon spends the least time moving through a sign at perigee, and the longest at apogee.

The Nodal Cycle — Moon and Ecliptic Plane

The planets revolve around the Sun in approximately the same plane, the ecliptic, and the Moon's orbit is tilted at a slight angle, about 5° to this plane. This means that each month the moon rises above and then sinks below the ecliptic. The two points at which it crosses the ecliptic are called nodes. When moving from south to north of the ecliptic, the Moon reaches its north node, and when moving from north to south, its south node.

The nodal cycle

The name ecliptic comes from the fact that eclipses happen when Sun, Moon and Earth are in line and on this plane. When the Moon becomes New close to a node, there will be a solar eclipse, and when it becomes Full close to a node, there will be a lunar eclipse. A solar eclipse draws a thin pencil of darkness on the Earth, where its zone of totality is confined. A lunar eclipse, in contrast, is a reddish shadow that passes across the Moon and is visible from half the Earth.

The north and south nodes were called dragon's head and dragon's tail respectively, indicating a belief that they were two special power points in the Moon's orbit – as if a menacing dragon were curled round the zodiac, liable to swallow the Sun at some unpredictable moment. A traditional British gardening guide advised people to avoid sowing seeds over the dragon's tail, the south node. This calendar, in common with bio-dynamic calendars, makes no distinction between these two lunar moments, avoiding both for its sowing times.

The Moon Riding High

How high does the Moon climb in the sky each night? The winter Full Moons are almost overhead, whereas through the summer they hang low above the horizon. On one day each month the Moon arcs highest across the sky, remaining above the horizon for the longest time, then a fortnight later it sinks to its lowest height above the horizon. There is a strong US lunar-gardening tradition that refers to these two halves of the month as 'riding high' and 'riding low'. The effect is very latitude-dependent so that readers in more northern countries will find this cycle more pronounced. For example, in Scotland the Moon hardly sets at one end of the month, then a fortnight later it hardly rises.

This monthly cycle mirrors the Sun's annual journey: in mid-winter the Sun remains low above the horizon, being in front of the stars of Sagittarius, whereas in mid-summer it climbs high in the sky, being in the opposite constellation of Gemini. This cycle fades away near the Equator, then in the southern hemisphere is reversed with both Sun and Moon rising highest against the stars of Sagittarius.

Bio-dynamic calendars also use this cycle, but label it differently. The cycle is split into ascending and descending, according to the height of the Moon above the observer's horizon. The planting out of seedlings is then recommended in the descending half. This cycle is just the 27.3-day star-month, but gets confused with that of the waxing and waning Moon, which may account for similar recommendations being ascribed to the waxing Moon period in British and American folklore.

Harvest Moon

The September Full Moon is called the Harvest Moon. Seen through autumnal mists, it often assumes a yellow hue and, remaining close to the horizon, it appears large in the sky and provides extra hours of illumination – precious to the farmer at this time of year.

At the autumnal equinox, the ecliptic (the path that the planets take round the Sun) is tilted at its least angle to the horizon. So the zodiac belt, containing the orbits of the Moon and planets, runs low above the horizon. This causes the Moon to rise only about 12 minutes later each day – whereas on average throughout the year it rises about 50 minutes later each day. Thus, at this time of harvesting, the Moon continues to rise soon after sunset for a number of successive evenings.

The Harvest Moon was held to be responsible for the ripening of produce and, to the Romans, Diana's day fell at the time of the harvest Full Moon, when offerings were made to her to ensure the ripening of their fruits.

Use of a star-calendar has the advantage that it gives one a motivation for looking at the heavens. Anyone can recognise Orion and the Plough, but what about Taurus and Gemini? In the afterglow of sunset, if the Moon and one or two planets are visible, one can trace the ecliptic as a line through the sky along which the Sun, Moon and planets all travel. Most of what is used in this calendar is visible in the sky above your garden.

Tasting the Wine

Is there a time when wine tastes best? Newspaper headlines affirmed this back in 2009, with the publication of the little book *When Wine Tastes Best* by Maria Thun and her son Matteus. It seems that Fruit days accentuated flavour, while Flower days brought out aromatics. Therefore, half of the zodiac was 'good' for wine tasting. It was recommended that Root days should be avoided for tasting wine – yuk! Traditionally, the vine was ruled by the Sun, and this new finding helps us to appreciate its fiery essence. Headlines claimed, 'Supermarket chains check lunar calendar before inviting critics to drink'. Tesco revealed that it had already been using this method (tasting in the Fire-trigon) for the previous two years. The Wine Society at its annual get-together promoted the idea. One wine-taster said it solved his 'long-standing puzzlement' as to how a wine would taste so much better on certain days.

To test this theory, invest in a 'wine saver' device which is designed to keep a bottle fresh for a few days after it has been opened. There are several such gadgets widely and cheaply available. The Moon moves from Fire (Fruit day) into Earth (Root day) in two or three days, so open the bottle on a Fruit day, then a couple of days later try to remember how it tasted and sample it on a Root day. If you believe it doesn't taste so good, then you have a good reason for planning a party on a Fruit day! It may help to bring out the fiery excitement and sense of fun amongst your guests. While you're at it, why not order some Bio-Dynamic wine to see if it lives up to its reputation? It's said not to give a hangover the next day ...

Using the Star Zodiac

he sidereal zodiac, or zodiac of the stars, is composed of 12 equal 30°
divisions – a kind of 'best-fit' of a regular structure upon the irregular
constellations of the ecliptic. It is called sidereal to differentiate it from
the tropical zodiac that is used by astrologers. It derives from antiquity
and, as such, would have been used by the three magi of the New Testament.

In the fifth century BC, the Greek historian Herodotus went to visit the Chaldeans
of Mesopotamia, and must have gazed on the fabled hanging gardens of Babylon.
These were watered by an extensive, underground irrigation system, where now
there is only desert sand. He was mainly impressed by the sheer abundance of their
harvests – of grain, figs, olives and vines – and was concerned that the account he
gave of them would strain the credulity of his readers.

In that period, 25 centuries ago, the Chaldeans began using the zodiac divisions,
dividing the sky into 12 equal sectors to mirror a division of their year into 12
months each containing 30 days. Did the star-wisdom for which the Chaldeans
became renowned help them in their harvests? Whereas the modern zodiac is
anchored to the seasons of the year, for the Chaldeans it was fixed by various
bright stars. They were concerned with what they experienced of the night sky –
for example they recorded each time Venus appeared and disappeared from the
sky – and perhaps their more experiential attitude could be of value today.

Debates over the star-zodiac's position are only over a degree or so. It is
important in some contexts but immaterial for a lunar-gardening calendar. There
were certain stars that fixed the zodiac position, in particular Spica, the bright star
signifying the sheaf of corn held by the Virgin, around 29° of Virgo. The star-zodiac

was used by the astrologers of antiquity in countries around the Mediterranean, until the fifth century AD. A different tradition then developed in the Muslim Arab world using the tropical zodiac, when the two zodiac systems were only a few degrees apart.

The Four Elements – Earth, Air, Fire and Water – had been used in Greek medicine and philosophy for seven centuries until, in the second century AD, after Claudius Ptolemy's time, they were absorbed into the fabric of the zodiac. The sky-triangles (trigons) were thus established, linking the four elements.

Memory of the sidereal zodiac became lost in Europe but continued in India; the zodiac used there is much the same as that understood by the ancient world. Thus the primal star-zodiac, from which the modern tropical zodiac evolved, has been in continuous use for over two millennia. It was rediscovered at the end of the nineteenth century, when clay tablets dug up from the banks of the Tigris were deciphered. A sidereal ephemeris was published in 1981 by Neil Michelson of the US Astro-computing Services. The present calendar uses the same reference as did Michelson, taking the 'Bull's Eye' star Aldebaran as being 15° of Taurus.

In the twentieth century, two incompatible lunar-gardening traditions burgeoned, both ignoring the sidereal zodiac. They offered a choice, of *either* using the tropical zodiac, as favoured nowadays by astrologers, or using 12 unequal constellations, as found in bio-dynamic calendars.

Use of the Tropical Zodiac

The first edition of *Planting by the Moon* explained how the tropical zodiac might be appropriate for human fate, while emphasising that evidence pointed to the sidereal as the right zodiac to use for plant growth:

'Incidentally, we are not implying that astrologers should be using the sidereal zodiac for their work. Rather, it seems that different phenomena may be attuned to different systems. The tropical zodiac is a moving zodiac, moving around 1° every 72 years against the fixed stars, and this evolving system may be valid for man. However, plants are simpler in their organisation than man, and have a far longer history, two factors which seem to have inclined their response to the Moon in terms of the more primal and unchanging sidereal zodiac. The position of the Moon in the tropical zodiac requires calculation, whereas its position in the sidereal zodiac can be observed in the sky. Although plants do not respond to the tropical zodiac divisions, it may well be that man's being is more in tune with the special mathematical treatment of time and space on which the tropical system depends.'

In simple terms: without an ephemeris (a prepared, printed table giving star times and calculations), could one discern when the Moon was entering into a tropical zodiac sign? Certainly not without a most difficult calculation. If we can only do it by calculation, how could one expect the instinctive plant realm to respond to a tropical ingress? In contrast, growers using our calendar have the advantage of being able to see in the sky what is happening in the book.

Agriculturally, the tropical zodiac shows the Sun's journey through the seasons in the northern hemisphere. Thus, the glyph or sign for Aries signifies the young seedling emerging in spring, then the next sign Taurus, the Bull, signifies the vigour of spring. The Sun's entry into Leo at the height of summer indicates its strength there, followed in September by the Virgin as a Ceres figure signifying the harvest. After that comes Libra, as the harvest is measured out; and then the Scorpion signifies the dying and decomposition of nature.

Interpreting the evidence of field experiments in terms of a zodiac framework hinges on the four-element symbolism. Thus, experiments show that root crops such as potato or radish grow better when the Moon is in front of one of the three Earth sectors of the sidereal zodiac. In terms of the tropical zodiac one would have to say that they were growing best when the Moon was in front of one of the three Air signs, because the shift between the two systems is nowadays almost one sign, or about 25°. This would not have the same symbolic significance as associating them with the Earth signs. Likewise it makes more sense to associate leaf crops such as lettuce with Water (sidereal) than with Fire (tropical). The four stages of plant growth – Root, Leaf, Flower and Fruit-seed – are associated with the four elements – Earth, Water, Air and Fire – *only* if a sidereal reference system is used.

The relationship between the sidereal and tropical zodiacs against the constellations

Almanacs based on this 'zodiac of the seasons' – the tropical zodiac – tend to advocate that the three Water signs are fruitful while the three Fire signs are barren, based on straightforward analogy or symbolism. It amounts to viewing only one-quarter of the zodiac as fertile. Sometimes the Earth signs are also admitted to be fertile.

Using the Bio-dynamic Calendar

A major alternative system to the one used here is that used in bio-dynamic calendars. Whereas the sidereal zodiac uses 12 equal divisions, the actual constellations associated with them vary in size, from huge Virgo (46°) to little Libra (18°). These irregular divisions are used by bio-dynamic calendars and differ from those used here for one-sixth of the time (some 60° in the circle of the zodiac).

Bio-dynamics developed within the anthroposophical movement founded by Rudolf Steiner which had drawn up its own 12-fold division of the heavens, loosely based upon the divisions made by the International Astronomical Union in 1928. The astronomers then decided to map out 13 constellations as lying on the ecliptic (Ophiucus, the Serpent-Bearer, being the thirteenth). The anthroposophists wanted no truck with this, however, and reconstructed a zodiac of just 12 constellations. Whereas the astronomers saw Libra as being 23° in length along the ecliptic, the anthroposophists gave it a mere 18°.

Sidereal and tropical zodiacs allocate equal spaces to each sign, but Steiner and his followers attempted to reflect astronomical reality more closely. The constellations by which they divided their calendar are therefore, by their very nature, unequal in size.

There was no great harm in any of this; indeed it was quite audacious. The trouble began when Maria Thun imposed the four elements on to this irregular set-up in the 1950s. Her use of these divisions made for a radical imbalance in the four elements. Root days (Earth) were assigned over 50 per cent more of the month than the Flower days (Air). The Air-constellation Libra is very short, while the Earth-constellation Virgo is two and a half times longer. The system was badly out of kilter, but nobody seemed to mind.

The Sidereal Zodiac

The present calendar uses the zodiac of the stars as the optimal reference that really works in an organic-growing set-up. Its basis is thus traditional, a framework tried and tested over millennia. The element rhythm of the star-zodiac is a simple thing, which is why plants respond to it. Just as investigation of lunar influence on plants is a recent phenomenon, so is the rediscovery of the sidereal zodiac in the West. Traditional gardening manuals have used the tropical zodiac without question, largely because it was the only one known to them. With the steady accumulation of evidence supporting the sidereal zodiac framework, the practice of lunar planting can now be established on a firm foundation.

The Rhythm of the Sun

We have lost our cosmos by coming out of our responsive connection with it, and this is our chief tragedy. What is our petty little love of nature – Nature! – compared to the ancient magnificient living with the cosmos and being honoured by the cosmos.

D. H. Lawrence

 or long-term planning in agriculture, there are two cycles that really count: an 18-year cycle of the Moon – of which more later – and the 11-year rhythm of the Sun, its sunspot cycle. If you look at a slice through an old tree trunk, you should be able to see how its rings become widest about every 11 years. The wider rings show increased tree growth. The beat to which trees, and a host of other living things, keep time is that of the changing level of solar activity, as indicated by the number of sunspots visible on the surface of the Sun. At the peak level of solar activity, the solar magnetic field, north and south of the ecliptic, flips over once per 11 years, creating a complete 22-year cycle. A maximum of sunspots then reflects this peak in magnetic turbulence. Both 11-year and 22-year cycles have an effect on the Earth.

The solar cycle, sunspot activity 1900–2000

The Solar Rhythm in Agriculture

While lunar rhythms define optimal sowing days within one season, this grand pulse of the Sun determines the years of peak production – and also lean years. This expansion and contraction rhythm within the Sun affects rhythms of total crop production, and much else besides. Experts generally assume that this influence is an indirect one via the Sun's effect on climate: electrical and magnetic changes in the upper atmosphere around the Earth are caused by solar radiation, and these affect the climate, which in turn affects crop yield.

Ever since the astronomer William Herschel stated two centuries ago that the price of wheat varied with the sunspot cycle, scientists have been arguing as to whether the effect is really present. Meteorologists at the Appleton Laboratories in Slough, England, researched the subject, and their conclusions were quite positive. Led by Dr J.W. King, they found that in Britain root-crop yields of potato, turnip and swede tended to peak at years of sunspot maxima, and also that rainfall tended to increase during those years.

The scientists further found that the number of days per growing season (defined as days with a mean temperature above 6°C/43°F) increased markedly during years of peak activity. This confirms the observations of an English farmer Mr Farrar, reported in *Farmer's Weekly* in 1975, that the length of his cows' annual grazing season varied markedly with the sunspot cycle. Family records showed that his cows stayed out to graze longest in years of peak sunspot activity, presumably reflecting a longer growing period of the grass.

An effect on mean temperature over the sunspot cycle was also found for the US states Maryland, Delaware and Virginia (1900-60), which showed mean variations of 2-3°C/4-5°F linked with the solar rhythm – although this correlated primarily with the 22-year cycle rather than the 11-year cycle. This has relevance, Dr King argued, for energy budgeting as regards fuel consumption.

Can farmers expect bumper harvests in years of sunspot maxima and more meagre yields in years when the Sun is quiet? More research is needed on Sun–Earth links before such recommendations can be made, but it may not be long before farmers take account of this solar pulse when planning ahead.

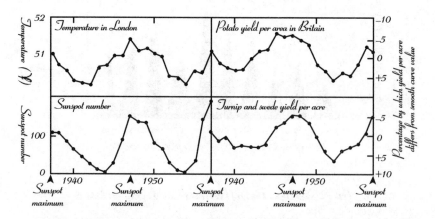

Variations in temperature, sunspot activity and yields of potatoes, turnips and swedes through two complete sunspot cycles (after King et al., 1974)

The effect of sunspot activity is also geographically dependent. Since most wheat is grown in the northern hemisphere and yields are increased in years of peak activity, global wheat prices tend to be lower at those times. King found modulations of 10–50 per cent in production in China, the US and the former Soviet Union. The solar cycle may be more evident in northern latitudes, where a greater flux of energised solar particles can funnel down into the atmosphere, as shown in the aurora borealis. In the southern hemisphere the cycle is reversed, with least growth in years of sunspot maxima. Dr King and others have suggested this as a basis for global economic planning.

Overall rainfall is also linked to the sunspot cycle. Dr R.G. Vines in Australia found that years of drought in certain countries are linked to troughs in the sunspot cycle, and also that large forest and prairie fires occur more often in these years. He counted bad fire-years as those on which losses overall due to fires were of one million acres or more. It is perhaps not surprising that fires on Earth should be linked to rhythms in the fiery energy of the Sun. Major US droughts seem to remain in step with the 22-year rather than the 11-year cycle.

Other phenomena have been shown to vary with the Sun's cycle. For example, years of peak activity seem to produce good wines. This appears both for French Burgundy and for German Rhine wines. The Russian expert Professor Alexsander Chizhevsky studied the relationship of the sunspot cycle to human history, claiming that more political upheavals, unrest and warfare took place in years of peak activity. Modern radio and electrical communication companies take a practical interest in the cycles of the Sun because they get more disturbance and interruption during times of solar storms.

When the Moon blots out the Sun during a total eclipse and the sky grows dark, the red rim of the solar chromosphere appears around the edge. This chromosphere, on years of sunspot maxima, will glow all around the Moon, whereas on quiet years of sunspot minima it is seen to glow each side of the Moon's black rim only at low solar latitudes. This means that, although normally invisible, the Sun's chromosphere expands and contracts over the 11-year cycle.

The Nutation Cycle

In the 1980s, reports started appearing of the 18.6-year lunar-node cycle present in climatic and agricultural records, and it is now viewed as being at least as influential as the solar pulse. Rainfall or drought is linked with this node or nutation cycle, in several parts of the world, for example the monsoons of India, tidal waves in the Earth's oceans, and the 19-year cycle in the flooding of the Nile.

The US cycles expert Dr Robert Currie has found that droughts in the US Midwest are caused by the 18.6-year node cycle. It affects atmospheric tides, which in turn influence the flow of rain-bearing air to the Midwest region. This area, where much of the world's grain is grown, is well known to suffer severe droughts about every 20 years. High-yield periods in the US, almost free of drought, tend to occur near minimum declination. The El Niño weather pattern, a global reverberation in climate affecting atmospheric perturbation, droughts and so on, also appears to be strongly linked to this nodal cycle.

Currie found that these cycles – 18.6 and 11 years – are both present in the atmosphere, the lunar signal being stronger than the solar. He has traced the 18.6-year cycle through floods and droughts in China for the past five centuries.

As with the sunspot cycle, half the cycle can often appear as the effective length. For example, the lunar declination, which relates to how high the Moon rises in the sky, varies with the 18.6-year nutation cycle; however, eclipses take 9.3 years, half the nutation cycle, to revolve around the seasons of the year, there being no difference between the north and south nodes in this regard. There is a 9.3-year cycle in US grain production and prices, with high corn yields occurring in years of minimum declination, while the lowest agricultural prices tended to occur every 18.6 years. Currie has also argued that a crop production cycle of 18.6 years exists. US pig, chicken and egg production also varies with the node cycle: 100,000,000 more chickens were produced in the US at the peak than the trough between 1910 and 1960 – the largest lunar influence yet identified. Herschel's original comment on corn prices and the rhythm of the Sun may therefore be adjusted to match more of a lunar than a solar rhythm.

The effects of these cycles has serious implications for global food production, and hopefully increased knowledge will lead to them being used in long-term agricultural and economic planning.

A Quiet Sun and Global Cooling

As of February 2013, the new sunspot maximum seems very lethargic. It was supposed to peak in 2015 but the solar experts did not see much sign of it. This is the sixth year of this cycle 'number 24', and we've experienced five years of colder winters. The previous minimum of 2005–2006 saw some of the quietest solar weather ever. Some experts believe that the present weak solar maximum augurs a future era of global cooling. The solar expert Dr Theodor Landscheidt told me this years ago in relation to this decade and I could not believe him! The Sun is not putting out strong solar flares, its sunspot numbers are low, and the solar wind pressure is also low so don't hold your breath for any big sunspot maximum. For reading on this subject, I would recommend *Chill, a Reassessment of Global Warming Theory* by Peter Taylor, who was quite influenced by Dr Landscheidt.

The Moon and Crop Yield

To speake then of the outward and active knowledge which belongs to our English Hous-wife ... Shee shall also know the time of the yeere, moneth and Moone, in which all hearbes are to be sowne; and when they are in their best flourishing, that gathering all hearbes in their height of goodnesse, shee may have the prime use of the same ... In February in the new of the Moone shee may sow Spyke, Garlicke, Borage, Buglose, Chervyle, Coriander, Gourds, Cresses, Marjoram, Palma Christi, Flower-gentle, white Poppy, Purslan, Radish, Rocket, Rosemary, Sorrell, Double Marigolds and Time. The Moone full shee may sow Anisseedes musked, Violets, Bleets, Skyrrits, White Succory, Fennell and Parslie. The Moone old sow Holy Thystell, Cole Cabadge, white Cole, greene Cole, Cucumbers, Harts Horne, Diers Grayne, Cabadge, Lettice, Mellons, Onions, Parsnips, Larkes Heele, Burnet and Leekes.

Gervase Markham, *The English Hous-wife*, 1615

 hereas the phase or synodic cycle is related to the general growth of a plant, it is the sidereal cycle that is mainly linked to the final crop yield. A sidereally based rhythm applies to one instant in a plant's life, when the seed is sown on moist ground and its growth begins. At this critical moment, when DNA starts to duplicate, it is the Moon's position against the zodiac that influences how the seed's potential will come to fruition.

Systematic investigation of how the time of sowing affects final growth really started with the experiments of Maria Thun in Germany in 1956 (*see also* page 13). This method had been followed in investigations in Steiner's anthroposophical society since the 1930s, but it was Thun who had the idea of picking out the element rhythm rather than the separate Moon–zodiac constellations.

One row of seeds was sown every few days, each time the Moon reached the middle of a new zodiac constellation, so that 12 rows were sown in the course of one revolution of the Moon around the zodiac, usually in May. Each of these rows was then allowed to grow for the same period of time and, after harvesting, the weights of the crops from each row were compared. Results for potatoes have been published since 1972 (co-authored with statistician Dr Hans Heinze) but other crops have been subjected to the same research.

Thun's research garden, located in a small, tranquil village surrounded by hills near Marberg in Germany, carries on this work. Over the decades she has developed a remarkable insight into the way in which cosmic influences affect crop yield. The dominant effect emerging from her trials related to a four-fold pattern in the zodiac, which allocates each of the 12 constellations to the four elements, as described on pages 10–11. For potatoes, maximum yields occurred in the three rows which were sown on Root days, when the Moon was in front of one of the three zodiac constellations traditionally associated with the Earth element, while minimum yields tended to occur when the Moon was standing in one of the Water constellations. The yield increases obtained were in the region of 30 per cent for the three Earth-element sowings as distinct from the other nine.

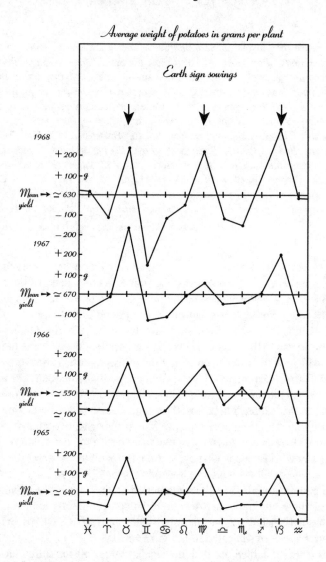

Potato yields according to the experiments of Maria Thun (1979)

Other studies using a similar experimental procedure have confirmed this four-element theory. Ulf Abele at Giessen University, as part of a doctoral study of bio-dynamic farming methods, tested barley, oats, carrots and radish during 1970-4, sowing 12 rows over the course of a month for each year. His barley and oats gave yields increased by 7 per cent overall when sowings were made on Fruit-seed (Fire) days, while his carrots and radish averaged a 21 per cent yield increase on the Root-day sowings (related to Earth).

Barley yields according to Abele (1973)

A German study by Ursula Graf investigated the Moon–zodiac rhythm for different soils. Over the three years 1973-5, potato and radish crops were investigated and yield increases were usually found for Root-day sowings as the theory predicted. However, this occurred only in crops grown on organically cultivated soil to which no chemicals had been applied, and not in crops grown on soil treated with synthetic fertiliser. Graf's conclusion was, *The soil seems to be a decisive factor in the occurrence of connections between Moon–zodiac constellations and crop yields'*, a view which directly echoes Thun's comment in 1964:

'I came to the conclusion that mineralised soils hardly reacted to these cosmic rhythms and their fine influences, whereas a humus-filled soil of whatever soil type was a good mediator for these forces.'

In other words, only organic gardeners are going to reap important benefits from the calendar and method of working used here. Soil quality is very relevant to the way lunar influence will show up and may account for variations in results achieved.

In Britain in 1976, Reg Muntz, a market gardener in Sussex, planted 24 rows of potatoes over two sidereal months. The results showed a mean yield increase of 25 per cent for rows sown on Root days compared to other sowings. Other trials by Muntz, which I helped to design, involved beans, carrots and lettuce. Maximum yields consistently showed up in the element trigons, whereas there was little indication of a lunar-phase effect.

Some thorough experiments were done in Wales over three years by Colin Bishop, amateur gardener and astrologer. In 1976, he planted 36 rows of lettuce over three months and achieved the results shown below. The average weight of the lettuce tops increased by about 50 per cent for those rows sown on Water-element (Leaf) days when compared with sowings made on other days. A repeat of the experiment in 1977 produced substantially the same results. In 1978, Bishop experimented with daily sowings of radish and again found that the relevant days, in this case Root days, produced the highest yield by 45 per cent. None of these data-sets showed a Moon-phase effect on crop yields.

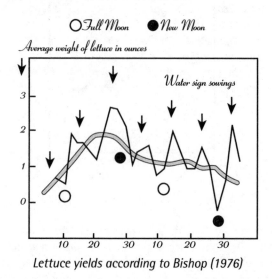

Lettuce yields according to Bishop (1976)

There is skill involved in growing rows of vegetables uniformly so that they aren't eaten by birds or slugs, and that lettuce form their hearts without bolting. Such uniform growth conditions are vital for the data to mean anything. Overall, in 1975–86, Muntz and Bishop grew some 400 rows of different vegetables in such trials and the net yield increase from sowing in the predicted trigons was 22 per cent. The soil used was not especially rich. The British results formed the groundwork for putting forward the calendar used here.

In 1980, J. Lücke sowed, as part of a doctoral thesis at the University of Giessen, four different plots of potatoes, with 12 rows per plot, one per Moon constellation. His Root-day yields were significantly in excess of the others, just as yields from the Leaf-day sowings were the least.

Sometimes a low-amplitude effect is observed, as in the extensive trials designed by Dr Hartmut Spiess. In three years of carrot trials 1979–81 at Dottenfelder farm near Frankfurt his yields averaged 8 per cent more on Root days, a small but significant increase as he undertook many sowings. The plot used was in an industrialised region of Germany where one might expect any sidereal-rhythm effects to be diluted. Some degree of scepticism has developed amongst bio-dynamic experts in Germany over the Thun model, focusing on the Spiess results as if they had failed to confirm the sidereal rhythms. I've gone into print arguing that they are low-amplitude effects and not null results. But let's agree with Spiess that:

The magnitude of the yield deviations that were associated with lunar factors was of practical significance.'

For a practical, Australian view of how to use the sidereal rhythms we may quote from the lectures of Alex Podolinsky:

The market gardeners may have noticed the best beans you have ever picked are on plants that are not huge and have not all that many leaves ... Now if you sow beans under a "leaf" zodiac sign, then they turn out such huge plants and they have very poor fruit. When you sow under a "seed" sign, you don't have all that much foliage (the plants don't need it, anyway) but they do have a lot of fruit. For pumpkins, in our experience, sowing under Leo is the most desirable ... We have run such trials and we have had roughly four times as many pumpkins in roughly the same acreage sowing them under Fruit rather than under Leaf.'

A Quality Test

Is the taste of a crop, as well as weight yield, affected by the trigons? Jack Temple, the well-known *Here's Health* organic-gardening correspondent, performed such a test in the spring of 1982, using the Thun sowing calendar:

'Every time a Leaf-sowing date turned up I sowed a row of lettuce and a row of radishes, and every time a Root-sowing day featured in her calendar we also sowed both lettuce and radish again. Then, when the directors and students from the Henry Doubleday Research Association dropped in on their yearly visit we put the trial to the test.'

Initially, Jack's visitors were shocked by this outlandish notion, so his reputation with them was at stake.

'However, all that disappeared as I put my knife through two radishes. One was juicy and the other had the texture of cotton wool. The juicy one had been sown on the correct day, a Root day, and the pithy radish had been sown on a Leaf day. That was not all: the juicy radish was ten weeks old while the pithy one was only eight weeks old. Both radishes were also tasted for quality and flavour.

Subsequently further sowings were tested. Each time we had the same result. Radishes sown on Leaf days were pithy and radishes sown on Root days were firm and fleshy. The lettuce trials did not produce quite such clear evidence, but lettuce sown on Leaf days were slower to bolt than those sown on Root days.'

To date, the evidence from such sowing trials demonstrates an effect caused by the primary element rhythms of the zodiac, but not for specific signs, as if plants, being simpler in their organisation than people, respond to this less-differentiated rhythm embodied in the zodiac. The weight of evidence to date indicates that the Thun model is valid and that the final yield of crops, when sown in good, organic soil, is related to the Moon's position according to the sidereal zodiac sign-element at the time of sowing.

The Lunar Nodes

There is at present less evidence for the effects of the lunar nodes on plants. According to Thun, the influence of the two nodes is liable to interfere with plant growth and to weaken the viability of seeds from plants sown at these times.

At perigee, when the Moon draws nearest to the Earth, the tides are pulled higher, rising some 30 per cent more than at apogee. It has been claimed that perigee is linked with stress. Thun has claimed that the apogee position causes sowings to sprout up rather quickly – which may not necessarily be beneficial for fruit formation – whereas the perigee position tends to inhibit growth. Evidence for the supposed adverse effect upon growth of perigee remains scant.

Sowing and Harvesting in the Phase Cycle

Does sowing at some point in the phase cycle produce better crops? Widespread folk traditions have suggested that it does. Modern experiments have been equivocal, though field experiments by Mather at the John Innes Horticultural Foundation in 1940 showed a consistent 15 per cent yield increase for maize and tomatoes sown on the second lunar quarter, confirming the hypothesis that the gardener had wished to test – the view that Kolisko had just published in *Agriculture of Tomorrow* (1939). Despite this confirmation, the author of the report was quite dismissive of his results. Crop-yield sowing trials that I've seen or been involved in have failed to detect much by way of any Moon-phase effects on crop yield. A comment by Thun on this issue is of interest:

'The influence of the Full Moon, throughout all the years of our research, only brought higher yields when these had been forced by mineral fertilisers or unrotted organic manures.'

Moonrise

A very thorough lunar-gardening experiment by Colin Bishop in 1978 used radish, sowing two rows in the morning and another two in the afternoon for over a month. The weight-yields did follow the star rhythm, peaking on Root days, but in addition there was a daily rhythm. The graph plots the Moon's motion against the horizon, centred on Moonrise. This graph was possible because Colin Bishop noted the time of each sowing, and also watered each row before inserting the seed – each morning on his way to work and then each afternoon as he returned. This means that the seed started growing as it was inserted into the soil. This is important if we are to take seriously the result: the hour of Moonrise showed up as the largest-amplitude effect in this data-set.

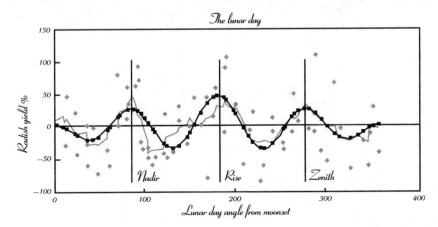

The lunar day, with Bishop's radish yields (1978)

There used to be a fine gardening column in *The Astrologer*, a London-based monthly of Victorian England, which always gave the time of Moonrise and recommended it be used for important gardening operations. Our calendar carries on this British tradition. My own opinion is that it is a very significant moment in the day when contemplating seed sowing or planting.

A New Year at Kew

Lunar-gardening research featured in the BBC2 programme *A New Year at Kew* in March 2007. Student Thea Pitcher of Kew's prestigious Royal Horticultural College had a plot allocated to her in 2006 for a research project of her choice. She decided to test this very book you are holding in your hand. Thea divided her plot into two, and sowed lettuce, sweet peas, onions, Swiss chard and leeks at 'right' and 'wrong' times.

On average, she told me, her lunar-planted vegetables showed about *30 per cent* more yield. It was an organic plot – Kew's Horticultural College favours organic methods whenever possible. Thea plans to write it all up for publication, and we may also see it featured on the website, www.plantingbythemoon.co.uk.

There was a BBC DVD available of all three series of *A New Year at Kew*, including the episode on Thea's work, which you may be able to find from second-hand sellers.

The Moon and Fertility

*The thirteenth of the waxing month
Is a bad day to start seeding
But the best for transplanting.*

Hesiod, Works and Days

here seems little doubt that the lunar cycle influences the life processes of plants', wrote Dr Bernard Dixon, former editor of the *New Scientist*. Dr Dixon was referring to the Moon-phase cycle which affects many of the growth processes in a plant – metabolic rate, absorption of water and nutrients, rate of growth and electrical activity have all been observed to fluctuate in accordance with this rhythm. This is of enormous significance to farmers and gardeners.

The Phase Cycle and Plant Growth

The rate at which seeds germinate in relation to lunar phase was first studied systematically in the 1930s by Kolisko, who concluded that wheat germinated faster when sown at Full Moon than at New Moon. Confirmation of this result appeared in studies by M. Maw, funded by Canada's Department of Agriculture, on the rate at which cress germinated. Over a six-month period, batches of cress grown in water usually germinated quickest at Full Moon and slowest at New Moon, the difference in rate being very marked.

Traditionally, it has always been assumed that sap rose up into plants and trees maximally during the Full Moon. Therefore activities such as tree felling should be performed at New Moon, and crops would preserve best if harvested at New Moon, due to their minimal water content. While direct evidence from studies of sap in trees and shrubs is scant, a study by Professor Frank Brown and Carol Chow investigated day-to-day variations in the absorption of water by bean seeds under temperature-controlled conditions at their laboratory in North-western University, Illinois. Each day, the amount of water the seeds absorbed over a four-hour period was measured. Large maxima were found to occur just before the Full Moon, absorption being on average 35 per cent higher than at New Moon.

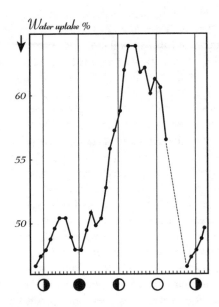

Water uptake by bean seeds (after Brown and Chow, 1973)

Biochemist Dr Harry Rounds at Wichita State University in the US reported that stress hormones in the blood of mice and men decreased sharply at Full and New Moon. He then extracted similar stress-related, 'cardio-acceleratory' substances from the leaves of various plants, especially geraniums, and found that their potency changed sharply for a short period following the Full and New Moon. His research is relevant to traditional advice that medicinal herbs should be picked at such times.

An important biochemical study was reported in 1989 from the University of Paris. It concerned a lunar pulse in plant DNA. Plant chromosomes, inside the nucleus of every cell, are large – much bigger than for animal cells. Two different types of structure were reported from x-ray studies. One, whose function is more related to storage of carbohydrates, was more developed at New Moon. Another type, more closely related to flowering and growth functions, was more developed at the Full Moon. This DNA response in plants is relevant to the traditional connection of the lunar cycle with fertility and growth.

A plant's metabolism can be assessed by how much oxygen it absorbs from the air. This was investigated in the classic experiments of Professor Frank Brown, in which potatoes and carrots were maintained in the dark over quite long periods, with the ambient conditions of temperature, humidity and pressure held constant. Through the years, he patiently charted over a million hours of potato time! From this, it emerged that the potatoes, although sealed from all light, were not at all in the dark about the cycles of the Sun and Moon. The Moon's daily rising and culmination (reaching its highest point in the sky) appeared as the hours of maximum metabolic rate for these root vegetables. In addition, their metabolic rate waxed and waned with the monthly lunar cycle: potato metabolism over the two weeks around the Full Moon was on average 15 per cent higher than that around the New Moon. For carrots the figure was 11 per cent.

A growing plant builds up an electrical field around it, in which the electrical potential at its top differs from that at the ground. This was investigated by Harold Burr, a professor at the Yale University School of Medicine. Burr decided to record the electrical potentials of trees by placing electrodes into their trunks. The first thing he discovered was that fluctuations in potential were the same for all the trees he investigated over a large area. Surprisingly, these were apparently unrelated to fluctuations in barometric pressure, humidity or the weather. He then monitored the potential of a single beech tree over a nine-year period, and this clearly showed that the dominant rhythm was tidal – 14.7 days – and that it peaked at the Full and New Moons. Analysis of this experiment showed that the tree's electrical activity was also responding to the level of solar activity (sunspots) but that the lunar cycles were stronger than these solar effects.

Bees are well adapted to the lunar month in their flight activity. Counters were fixed to beehive entrances by M. Oehmke, a biologist at the Goethe University, Frankfurt. Through the course of the year, these showed a huge lunar fluctuation in bee activity. This varied between species, one species being at least twice as busy at New Moon as at the Full. Bee activity fertilises flowers, reminding us of the connection between the synodic cycle and fertility.

Nowadays when we speak of a month we forget the lunar origin of this term, and do not consider the life-rhythms in all living things linked to this monthly cycle. No doubt humans, in our mechanical environment, respond less to the cycle of the month then other living things. *'On the days of the Full Moon, something colossal is taking place on Earth'*, averred Rudolf Steiner, in his agriculture lectures of 1924. He added the vital corollary, *'these forces spring up and shoot into all the growth of plants, but they are unable to do so unless rainy days have gone before.'* Plants, in spite of man-made changes, still live and grow attuned to this primary cosmic rhythm. These various results show that in plant growth, various different rhythms are related to the Moon's monthly cycle and that the time of Full Moon is especially important for them. Around this time a plant's metabolic rate and water absorption are at their greatest.

We have seen how laboratory studies indicate that a higher rate and speed of germination is attained if seeds are sown just before or round the Full Moon and, to a lesser degree, if sown over the New Moon; also that seeds and plants absorb water optimally around this part of the lunar month. In countries where drought is endemic this would have some bearing on the success of a crop and may have reinforced the idea that all plants should be sown around Full Moon.

Full Moon and Animal Husbandry

Geld hogs, steers, rams and kids when the Moon is waning.
Pliny, *History of Nature*

It seems that even nowadays many farmers who have never heard of Pliny's recommendations still follow them regarding castration and other surgery on animals, fearing complications due to excessive bleeding at Full Moon. There is some medical evidence to support this practice: some years ago a doctor in the United States investigated a group of 1,000 operations which had been performed in his hospital. He noted the Moon's phase at the time of all the operations in which complications from bleeding had occurred and found that at least four times more occurred at Full Moon than at New Moon. He analysed other groups of operations and obtained the same striking result. From this data, it appears that the period around the New Moon is indeed the optimal time for such operations, and that the Full Moon period should definitely be avoided. Animals also bite more at the Full Moon, or so the *British Medical Journal* reported in December 2000!

Horse Breeding

... [farmers] notice the aspects of the Moon, when at Full, in order to direct the copulation of their herds and flocks, and the setting of plants or sowing of seeds: and there is not an individual who considers these general precautions as impossible or unprofitable.
Ptolemy, *Tetrabiblos*, Ch. III

In the Middle Ages, the Arabs were the finest horse breeders in Europe and the Near East. Their subtle understanding of astrology may well have helped them in this breeding process.

Like cows, horses ovulate every three weeks throughout the breeding season. The vets can tell within a day or two if conception has occurred, therefore the record of mare coverings is a record of their times of ovulation. There is a tendency for horses to become synchronised in their ovulation, and hence for the stud farm to become more busy at three-week intervals. In this they resemble many

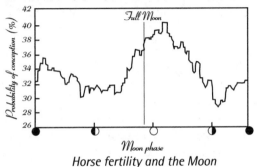

Horse fertility and the Moon

creatures in the wild, where the females tend to ovulate in synchrony. The diagram plots probability of conception at first covering around the lunar cycle (the data is smoothed with a 'moving average'). It clearly peaks on the days after Full Moon. Mare oestrus also tended to peak somewhere around Full Moon, being then in the region of 10 per cent more than at New Moon. In early 2005 my results on thoroughbred horse breeding and the lunar cycle, using 14 years of studfarm data, were published in *Biological Rhythm Research* (December 2004, 'Lunar Effect on Thoroughbred Mare Fertility', pp. 317–328). This clearly demonstrates, for the first time, the huge effect that the Full Moon exerts upon mare fertility and the modulation caused by the node cycle, which affects the strength of the Full Moon.

Harvest Time

Traditions link the time of harvesting crops to the Full or New Moons. One may believe that water and metabolic rhythms linked to this cycle should affect the final condition of a crop. Roman and Greek beliefs on this have already been touched upon. As an instance of modern awareness of lunar rhythms, here is the account of a Sydney-based company on the subject of their tomato harvest:

'We are growers of tomatoes, on a relatively large acreage, and found throughout the years that during the period of the Full Moon, a noticeable change takes place in the maturing and colouring of tomatoes. This quickening maturity, irrespective of temperature, only takes place two or three days before and after the Moon has reached its fullness.

During this period, marketplaces on the east and south coastal states have an influx of coloured fruit, where in normal times there is a high percentage of green and semi-coloured fruit. We have tested this out on many occasions and our statistics over many years have shown more fruit passing through our packing house through these periods, and that the fruit is much more forward in colour. These conclusions may well echo the experience of many growers.'

Such a clearly perceived effect reflects the more regular and predictable climate of Australia compared with Britain.

For crops that are to be dried, where juiciness and high water content are not required, at or just before New Moon seems the appropriate time for harvesting. Thus, the great French herbalist Maurice Messengé always picked his herbs at this time. He dried the herbs before use and believed that their virtue would preserve best if picked then.

Moonstamp for Timber

A related practice which can be traced back to antiquity is that of felling timber at the New Moon. The founder of the US Cycles Foundation in Pittsburgh described how in South America the Moon phase at which timber was felled was stamped on the wood, the idea being that New Moon timber preserves better and cuts more easily than that felled at Full Moon. French law from 1669 until the Revolution specifically required that timber be felled only during a waning Moon, a practice directly echoing the words of the Roman historian Plutarch:

'The Moon showeth her power most evidently in those bodies which have neither sense nor lively breath; for carpenters reject the timber of trees fallen in the Full-Moon as being soft and tender, subject also to the worm and putrefaction, and that quickly by means of excessive moisture.'

Accounts of this practice (discussed in Kolisko's *Agriculture of Tomorrow*) give the impression that the effect is more evident in tropical or sub-tropical regions. The experience of the Australian bio-dynamic farmer Alex Podolinsky is relevant:

'There is more water in trees and grass and all plants towards Full Moon than towards New Moon. In the old days, good timber cutters chopping down valuable timber would never cut other than towards the New Moon. They would not cut towards Full Moon, the timber was not as good. If we cut hay we also cut as much as possible towards New Moon and not towards Full Moon. We get much better quality hay that way.'

On the Trout Farm

It isn't just plants that have their fortnightly rhythms of growth. Trout in an aquarium grow to a rhythm whereby their weight peaks just before the Full and New positions. This was shown using several hundred small trout, and weighing them every four days – a commendably simple experiment.

Fish respond biochemically to the lunar cycle. Salmon and some species of trout hatch in fresh water and at a certain stage of their lives transform to become ocean-dwelling, salt-water fish. Salmon fisheries need to be able to predict this event as they have to release hatchery-reared fish into the river shortly before it occurs. The thyroid hormone thyroxine triggers this big moment in the salmon's life, and there is a specific New Moon in the spring which times this hormone surge. If the salmon wish to swim down the river without being seen by predators then a New Moon is the optimal time of month for them. This was discovered by zoologists at the University of California who concluded that a lunar calendar was essential for efficient culture of this economically valuable resource.

Back in the 1920s, an American called John Knight developed his theory about when to fish. He posited that fish feed only twice a day when the Moon either culminates (reaches its highest point) or reaches its nadir (lowest point below the horizon). For avid fishermen, the correct time to indulge their art can be calculated using our calendar. Six hours should be added to or subtracted from the given times of Moonrise. For the waning Moons, the calendar gives Moonset times, as they happen during the day

Gardening
Aspects

To the better furthering of the gardener's travails, he ought afore to consider, that the Garden earth be apt and good, wel turned in with dung, at a due time of the year, in the increase of the Moon, she occupying an apt place in the Zodiack, in agreeable aspect of Saturn, and well-placed in the sight of heaven ... for otherwise his care and pains bestowed about the seeds and plants, nothing availeth the Garden.

Thomas Hill, *The Gardener's Labyrinth*, 1577

s viewed from the Earth at Full Moon, the Sun and the Moon are said to be in opposition. Two weeks later at New Moon they form the aspect called conjunction. An aspect is an angle, measured around the ecliptic from the centre of the Earth, expressing a symmetry within the zodiac. In order of decreasing strength, the aspects are:

♂ conjunction (0°) ☌ solar eclipse (0°)

☍ opposition (180°) ☋ lunar eclipse (180°)

△ trine (120°)

☐ square (90°)

✶ sextile (60°)

The square and opposition are considered inhibiting and stressful, whereas the trine and the sextile are thought to be beneficial and harmonious.

Each month, the Moon forms similar angles or aspects with Saturn and with the other planets. The Moon–Saturn relationship seems to have particular importance to agriculture and the life of plants. Our calendar indicates most of the Moon–Saturn aspects as they occur, some Moon–Sun aspects when they are relevant, and all the aspects between Moon and Venus as they fall on Flower days. The Venus aspects are recommended for working with flowers – sowing, planting out and grafting. In his ever-popular *Herbal*, Culpeper gave advice about when to pick herbs in terms of finding the right celestial aspects:

'Let them be full ripe when they are gathered, and forget not the celestial harmony before mentioned; for I have found from experience that their virtues are twice as great at such times as others.'

Aspects to Saturn

The planet Saturn was traditionally viewed as important for farmers. The Roman god Saturn presided over agriculture (his name is thought to derive from the Latin sator, sower), and the Saturnalia, held just before the winter solstice, was a week-long, lively agricultural festival in memory of the Golden Age. Indeed classical writers have mentioned no other planet in this regard. In his agricultural poem *Georgics*, Virgil advised, 'Watch the transit of the cold star Saturn.' Saturn's sickle had a more rustic meaning before it came to denote the limitations of time. In astrological terms, Saturn represents life's challenging, defining and shaping principle. It is also sometimes depicted as Chronos, Old Father Time.

As an example of this traditional view, the sixteenth-century work on gardening lore, *The Gardener's Labyrinth*, explained about sextile aspects between Saturn and the Moon: 'it is then commended to labour the earth, sow, and plant' whereas, during the square aspect between these two, it was 'denied utterly to deal in such matters.' The trine was also approved, but the opposition was not.

Much the same advice featured in seventeenth-century British works, for example, *The Whole Art of Husbandry*, while *Dariotus Redivivus* advised that farmers:

'ought to have a special respect to the state and condition of Saturn, that he be not ... afflicted, because he hath chief dominion over husbandry and the commodities of the Earth; let him therefore (if you can so fit it) be in good aspect ... to the Moon.'

For planting crops, the general advice was: 'Plant what you intend, the Moon being either in conjunction, sextile or trine of Saturn.'

Modern bio-dynamic farmers also consider the lunar opposition to Saturn to be important, so for some time it was the only celestial aspect to feature in their calendar. It is interesting to note that the Foundation for the Study of Cycles, based in Pittsburgh, USA, has found a 29.8-year cycle in famines, a frequency which corresponds almost exactly with the average time it takes Saturn to make one complete revolution through the zodiac.

Our calendar gives the lunar aspects of conjunction, opposition, trine and sextile to Saturn for Leaf, Flower and Fruit-seed days, but not for Root days, as there would be little point in sowing trees and perennial crops on Root days. The harmonious times – trine and sextile – are suitable for sowing perennials and trees, through Saturn's association with long-term cycles, and for increasing the hardiness of plants. Stressful times – conjunction, opposition and square – should be avoided. However, readers may wish to test the belief of bio-dynamic farmers that the opposition is the best Saturn aspect to use.

All aspects are given to the nearest ten minutes GMT (or BST in summer). The best time to sow or plant is between one hour before and half an hour after the aspect occurs, although if that is impossible for practical reasons, sow within six hours before, rather than after the event.

Vines and the Sun

Readers with a warm and sunny spot in the garden may wish to try growing vines. For the ancients and for traditional astrological-rustic books, the vine had a solar rulership. The US biologist-astrologer Lee Lehman compared rulerships of all sorts of plants from a variety of traditional sources and she found a nucleus for which all her sources agreed. The vine was one of these. Most of these don't concern us, as planetary events are not given in the calendar (it would be too complicated). However, the main Sun–Moon aspects are given and these are the important options for when to establish a vine, particularly cutting the scion in autumn and grafting it in spring. These tasks should also be done on a Fruit-seed day.

The ancients also related wine quality to the movement of Jupiter around the zodiac. As it orbits once in 12 years, it enters a new zodiac sign each year. Various astrologers I consulted expressed surprise about the solar rulership of the vine, as they had expected it to be ruled by Jupiter. All those words associated with jovial derive from that sphere in the sky: Jupiter, or Jove. Those seriously considering setting up a vineyard might also research solar aspects to Jupiter or Venus.

To help understand this idea, let's quote from a recent book on plant rulerships by Jean Elliott which brought Culpeper's *Herbal* up to date. She gave the grapevine as solar in its rulership and summarised solar qualities as follows:

'The Sun: Core essence, integrated conscious self, playful self, vitality. Play, children; palaces and mansions; day; gold. The Sun rules Leo. Colour: yellow, orange, gold.'

Its section on plants ruled by the Sun reads:

'Grapevine: (Vitis vinifera). Lilly, Culpeper [referring here to two seventeenth-century astrologers who gave rulerships]. Either grows as a long-lived climber or in bush form for wine. Green/white flowers from early to midsummer. Grapes in Autumn. Under 'Vine' in Herbal. Brought to Britain by the Romans.'

Eighteen years ago, one of the most respected French wine estates, Clos de la Coulée de Serrant in Savennières, owned by Nicholas Joly, changed over to bio-dynamic principles. Under azure skies in the Loire valley, there are two wines now produced using a lunar calendar: Joly's and Noel Pinguit's Le Haut Lieu. The latter has won every award going (described as 'a stunningly intense, joyful wine' – solar qualities, perhaps). One per cent of French wine is currently produced according to a bio-dynamic regime. Joly expresses his views in rather solar terms:

'When we look at a flower or fruit, it becomes perfectly clear that they owe their beauty, their colour, their fragrance, their variety of shapes and flavours to the Sun. And it is precisely this power of expression, which manifests itself in constantly new variations, that must again be allowed to flourish again in wine – and in every foodstuff.'

As the grapes ripen, a critical situation develops in the last few weeks, crucial for final quality as the grapes have to be collected at optimal ripeness. As acidity gradually decreases, the sugar content rises. After harvesting, they are crushed and the mix poured into barrels. That moment needs careful choosing, being the 'birth-moment' of what will mature into wine, so make sure it's a Fruit day.

Maria Thun is collaborating with a wine-grower in the South of France. When I went to visit, her research plot of vines was being treated with various sprays of different copper concentrations. Copper sulphate is regularly sprayed on to vines as an insecticide, but she was using much weaker concentrations along the lines of homoeopathic medicines, to investigate their efficacy against infestation.

The year 1990 was a sunspot maximum, and is regarded as a classic wine year. The last maximum occurred in 2001. As the Sun expands, with solar flares extending further out from its surface and aurorae maximising at Earth's poles, are the best wines then formed? To quote from Gauquelin's classic, *The Cosmic Clocks*:

'According to the French Astronomical Bulletin, years in which the number of Sun spots is highest are great vintage years for Burgundy wines; in years with few Sun spots poor vintages are produced. The Swiss statistician A. Rima found similar results when he analysed the production of Rhine wines for the past 200 years.'

The Malignity of a Solar Eclipse

The great astronomer Johannes Kepler composed calendars that prognosticated for the year ahead and in one of them (1602) he explained how it all worked. He described an early version of the Gaia theory, whereby the Earth had a vegetable-animal force which had a sense of geometry, which enabled it to respond to the celestial aspects in terms of climate, harvests, good wine years and political stability. Kepler gave an analogy to explain how this worked: just as a peasant could take delight in the piping of a flute without knowing anything about the theory of musical harmony, so the Earth could respond in an unconscious way to the changing geometry of the heavens. The Earth more or less shuddered during an eclipse, he wrote:

'Eclipses ... are so important as omens because the sudden animal faculty of the Earth is violently disturbed by the sudden intermission of light, experiencing something like emotion and persisting in it for some time.'

Early tablets from ancient Babylon testified to the belief in the infertility of the land around the time of an eclipse. As a belief, it has endured longer than most. The early bio-dynamic sowing calendars by Franz Rulni advocated not sowing anything important for several days after an eclipse, while its successor, the modern Thun calendar, gives just the day of an eclipse as not good for planting.

In the Netherlands, there is a garden with a few ragged pear trees which only started to bear small, bitter fruit nine years after they were planted. As a test, they were deliberately planted at the inauspicious moment of a solar eclipse by Karen Hamaker-Zontag, the eminent Dutch astrologer. It would be interesting to see more tests done on this phenomenon.

That eclipses do diminish seed quality was demonstrated a few decades ago in a series of seed-germination experiments by Theodor Schwenck, which are summarised in his classic work, *Sensitive Chaos*.

The Organic Way

Clear the sheds of dung, but not at new moon or half moon.

Cato, *On Farming*

he sidereal rhythms described in this book will work optimally for the gardener using organic methods. An interest in lunar gardening goes hand in hand with organic growing. Organic soil can produce crops healthy enough to respond well to these cycles, whereas soil that has been chemically fertilised may not, or not to the same extent. Organic soil is built up over the years to be humus-rich with compost and well-rotted manure. If inorganic fertilisers are relied upon, on the other hand, these will force the growth of plants, initially increasing quantity but not quality, and decreasing storage life, disease resistance and soil quality.

Organic farming has been defined as growing crops free from herbicides, pesticides, fungicides and inorganic fertilisers. At one stage, organic growing was considered the province of cranks, but all that has changed, with a broader view of organic production as working in harmony with, rather than in opposition to, nature. With huge food surpluses from overproduction and farmers being paid to set aside productive land, it is an advantage that the organic way involves a slower rate of growth and a lower final crop yield, relying on natural rhythms and quality. While organic growing tends to be more labour-intensive, this can also be seen as a movement towards a community of workers. Working with the seasons is another advantage, as produce always tastes best when harvested and eaten at the right time.

A five-year study published by the US Department of Agriculture found that organic farms had yields roughly equal to, and costs considerably lower than, conventional farms. Organic farms used more labour per unit of produce, but consumed less energy. Panels of tasters tend to prefer organic food, and organic foods tend to have a longer shelf-life. The concept of quality is being refined by these and other investigations and should be of great relevance for future studies of lunar influence. We are moving towards a positive definition of what 'organic' means in terms of taste and other characteristics, and not merely the absence of chemical products.

The organic way also has advantages where livestock are concerned. Research in animal husbandry has confirmed that animals fed on organic diets are more fertile and less prone to disease. With human male fertility apparently continuing a long-established downtrend, this may have even broader implications. In the 1990s epidemic, no cows born and bred on organic farms got BSE. Indeed, bio-dynamic farms received a boost when a statement made in 1923 by Rudolf Steiner was unearthed: if cows were fed on meat produce, he said, they would go mad.

The Organic Market

The organic movement really took off during the 1980s, largely as a northern and middle-European phenomenon. There are 4,000 registered organic producers in the UK. Demand continues to grow at a phenomenal rate – organic sales had increased to £1.12 billion in 2003–2004. About 10 per cent of farmland in Austria, Denmark and Sweden is organic, while the figure is around 2 per cent in Germany, France, Italy and the UK. Almost 10 per cent of British organic farms are bio-dynamic and there are now about 50 such farms. Many organic farms are offering delivery services or supply through local farmers' markets, in order to allow more consumers to access their products, ensure seasonal produce and minimise transport of goods.

In 1993, an EU regulation laid down a legally binding standard of guidelines for organic farming which sufficed to block US legislation of 1998, permitting genetically modified, additive-treated and irradiated food to be sold as organic. The arrival of these new technologies poses rather urgently the question whether any kind of life-energy exists in food. Those with an interest in organic farming or lunar gardening must surely believe that it does.

Jack's Organic Garden

Jack Temple used to write the organic gardening section for *Here's Health* magazine and his columns were collated in his book, *Gardening without Chemicals*, which contained fascinating information about his gardening methods. He would also assure readers that sowing by the correct Moon element made a big difference, even for cress grown indoors: it was worth waiting a few days until the Leaf days came round, he reckoned, even if it meant storing the cress in the fridge for a while.

Jack was also an advocate of the organic principle. He would put calcified seaweed into his compost preparations, and also rock phosphate (from Chile). This is an inorganic chemical, but on the Soil Association's approved list because it is slow-release. Indeed, some gardeners don't like using it on the grounds that it is too insoluble.

After harvesting a vegetable plot, Jack wouldn't dig. He'd spread organic kitchen waste across the ground, with any vegetables the local shops were throwing out, then cut grass and nettles and a dusting of calcified seaweed. Then it was all covered with flattened cardboard boxes, and finally the plot was covered with black plastic sheeting to prevent weeds growing. Insects munched their way through beneath this, until in the spring the soil was friable and ready for the next crop. The taste of his vegetables was an experience.

The way he dealt with pests was also natural. There was an irrigation stream around his plot, which provided enough frogs to control the slugs. Once, a row of his beans was infested by blackfly. 'Needs some more compost', Jack remarked. He was proud of his worm-compost. What connection compost application was supposed to have with blackfly infestation was far from clear to me, but it was applied and the next week, the blackfly were gone. He seemed to have the right attitude towards harnessing the forces of nature to human ends: ingenious, yet with proper respect.

Foot-and-Mouth Epidemic

In the last week of February 2001, the world's worst foot-and-mouth epidemic hit the headlines just as Saturn was coming into conjunction with Algol (at 26° of Taurus), which has the reputation of being the most evil star in the firmament, while Saturn is traditionally associated with agriculture. Saturn remained within one degree of Algol throughout most of March, as the British farming industry saw the progress of the massive extermination project directed by computer projections in London, rather than the advice of recognised foot-and-mouth experts who were advocating a different course of action. Meanwhile, an outbreak in the Netherlands was coped with, swiftly and with few deaths, by inoculation.

It is interesting to note that both Saturn and Jupiter were then in the Taurus constellation. They were separating, having been conjunct the previous year. While only a tiny proportion of the cows slaughtered were actually diagnosed as having the disease, it is significant that hardly any organically reared cows were diagnosed from the foot-and-mouth outbreak, just as not one cow born and bred as organic suffered from BSE.

Monthly Tasks in the Vegetable Garden

... the powerful grace that lies
In herbs, plants, stones, and their true qualities.

Friar Lawrence, *Romeo and Juliet*, Act II

en Whyatt, who has spent many years using organic methods, has kindly provided this excellent and practical seasonal guide to organic vegetable gardening throughout the year. I hope it will prove useful to the reader, even though climates may not be quite the same as for Ken in south-west England. While this guide gives valuable advice on when to carry out tasks throughout the year, readers will need to refer to the calendar for day-to-day information on when best to sow, tend and harvest particular crops.

January

Burn woody rubbish in a slow, smother fire. Sieve the resultant ash and mix it with an equal quantity of leaf mould to make a wonderful base for sowing seeds later on. Keep the ash in a dry place. Stack clods of earth round the bonfire; these will crumble and make a useful ingredient in a potting mixture for tomatoes later in the spring.

Spread compost on vacant land to remain until the soil is suitable for making seed beds.

Inspect all vegetables in store and safeguard against hard frosts by covering with straw, matting or other light, dry material.

Make a cropping plan for your plot, making sure that cabbages (and members of the cabbage family) and potatoes are rotated by planting them in an area not occupied by these crops for at least two years.

Order your seeds in good time. Early potato seeds should be chitted – placed in trays in a light, frost-free place so that they develop short green shoots – thus gaining several weeks' growth at planting time.

If your soil is a sticky clay, do not walk on the garden unnecessarily unless it is frozen. Keep a supply of old planks to put down to walk on when you pick sprouts and other winter crops in wet weather. This will ensure that your soil will be easier to dig in the spring.

If you have a sheltered area facing south and the soil is well drained and crumbly, make some sowings of early peas and broad beans (long-pod varieties). Cloches will give added protection.

You can also plant shallots if the soil is not sticky.

February

Lightly fork over the area intended for sowings of early carrots, lettuce, cabbage, beetroot (red beet) and parsnips. Incorporate well-rotted compost or leaf mould and sieved bonfire ash in the top 5 cm/2 in. If the soil is too sticky to rake to a fine tilth, keep it covered with cloches for a week or so.

Make small sowings of early peas, short-horn carrots, lettuce, summer cabbage and Brussels sprouts.

Delay sowings of parsnips and beetroot (Boltardy is recommended) until late in the month and choose a sheltered spot. Even then, beet will require the protection of cloches. These seeds are large and can be spaced about 5 cm/2 in apart. A small sowing should provide salad beetroot in June.

Parsnips should be sown at intervals of about 23 cm/9 in, in rows 45 cm/18 in apart. Seed must be fresh and it is advisable to sow in groups of three or four seeds to ensure even germination, the weaker plants being thinned out in April. To ensure the rows are well marked (parsnips are slow starters), sow radish about 2.5 cm/1 in apart in the same rows. These will be ready for pulling long before the parsnips have grown large.

Jerusalem artichokes can be planted about 30 cm/12 in apart. Remember they can attain a height of almost 2 m/6 ft so they can be used as a wind break, as shade for late sowings of lettuce and as an excellent vegetable in their own right.

Make your main sowings of broad beans this month. It is worth planning to succeed broad beans by a crop that requires plenty of nitrogen, such as cauliflower, autumn cabbage or broccoli. The beans' roots increase the soil's nitrogen content. When the crop has been picked, cut the top growth to ground level and leave the roots where they are.

March

A busy month if the weather is reasonable. It is better to wait until the end of the month before sowing than to sow on pasty soil. Broad beans are a worthwhile crop, but must be given plenty of room to develop. Pinch off the top 15 cm/6 in when they are in flower – the shoots make a delicious salad or cooked vegetable and the plants are less liable to attack from blackfly.

Sow main-crop Brussels sprouts, cabbages and short-horn carrots for summer use; celery or celeriac and leeks in seed boxes in garden frames or greenhouses.

Plant out lettuces from February sowings, ensuring they have plenty of compost in drills directly under their roots. Further sowings of lettuce should be made from now throughout the spring and summer. A pinch of seed will sow a short row of about 1.2 m/4 ft and this will suffice if sowings are made fortnightly. The same rule applies to radish, which are large seeds and can be dropped in a drill singly about 2.5 cm/1 in apart.

Buy onions as sets – onions whose growth has been arrested in the autumn – and plant them in fine soil manured for a previous crop. Just push them into the soil without bruising them, and cover their necks. As they start to root, they may push themselves out of the soil. Replant them with the tip of a trowel.

Parsnips can still be sown, but should be in by the end of the month if they are to attain maximum growth.

Peas can be sown in continuation. The taller kinds will need the support of twigs or netting and the rows should be far enough apart to make picking easy. Rows of lettuce or radish can be sown as catch crops between the peas at the same time, as these will mature before the peas are ready and will benefit from some shade.

Fine soil with plenty of compost is needed for a good yield of early potatoes. If these have two or three green shoots already formed (see January) they can be planted towards the end of March.

Spinach, spinach-beet and Swiss chard can now be sown, the last being the most useful, its thick, fleshy mid-ribs making a separate dish from the large, spinach-like leaves.

Annual weeds, and even perennial ones, will wilt in the sun if the surface of the ground is hoed slightly. They may look unsightly for a while, but worms will assist in clearing them, and the dying material will act as mulch.

Continue to plant out Brussels sprouts, cabbages, savoys and broccoli. There is still time to plant marrows and cucumbers outdoors if plenty of humus is available to give them a good start.

Plant leeks from seed beds. Trim about 2.5 cm/1 in off the leaf tips and trim back straggly roots, then drop them into holes made by a dibber about 20 cm/8 in apart and water in without pressing back the soil.

Runner beans and tomatoes will require strong stakes, which are easier to push in if the ground is soaked first. Plant after the stakes are in position.

April

Tomatoes can be sown in late March, but plenty of light and an average temperature of 15–18°C/60–65°F is necessary for a good start, so early April is usually better. Minimum requirements are a warm window-sill not subject to draughts, a good seed compost in boxes of 5-cm/2-in depth and thin sowing. When the seedlings are about 5 cm/2 in high they should be planted in separate 9-cm/3½-in pots and grown until early May in a warm, light place before moving to a cold greenhouse. Do not plant outdoors until late May or early June.

A useful plant is land or American cress, similar in appearance, taste and food value to watercress. Sow in a damp spot such as the north side of a low wall, or close to a concrete path, where it is easy to keep them watered.

The main sowings of dwarf beans, beet, broccoli, spinach, autumn and winter cabbages, carrots and herbs of various kinds can be made this month (bearing in mind that dwarf beans are frost-tender, so these could be delayed to late April or even May). January King cabbage and the varieties of purple and white broccoli are useful winter vegetables which will withstand hard frosts when greens are so expensive to buy. Incidentally, broccoli and Brussels sprouts need an open situation and at least 60 cm/2 ft between plants, with a good firm soil. Wind tends to rock them, so draw up some surrounding soil from time to time to hold their stems firm.

Early and maincrop potatoes should be planted before the end of the month, giving the maincrops a minimum gap of 60 cm/2 ft in the rows and 75 cm/21/2 ft between the rows. If the early potatoes have come through the soil, earth them up slightly and cover with soil if frost threatens. Periodically, they should be earthed up, leaving a curved rather than a sharp ridge.

May

Take the opportunity during dull, showery weather to plant out seedling cabbages, cauliflowers and Brussels sprouts. Plant to the base of the lowest leaf stalks and make the soil really firm.

Plant out thinnings of lettuces but ensure the roots are not damaged. They must be thoroughly watered unless the weather is showery, and prefer a spot with some daytime shade.

Runner beans, courgettes, marrows and ridge cucumber are all sown this month, but must have some protection from late frosts. Cloches are ideal for this and home-made polythene frames or tunnels ensure a good start. Close up the ends with a sheet of glass, as wind-tunnels are not appreciated by any plant.

Early May is the best time for sowing maincrop beetroot, the thinnings of earlier sowings being useful raw in salads. Pick them when they are the size of a golf ball.

Late broccoli, savoys and winter cabbage, such as the excellent January King, are sown this month. Swedes and turnips are useful as a winter crop and should be thinned to 20 cm/8 in apart when 2.5 cm/1 in high.

Capsicums sown in the middle of May, given sufficient warmth, will provide green pods in the autumn.

It's not too late to sow carrots; in fact, the later sowings are less prone to attack from carrot fly. Incidentally, when thinning carrots for salads, remove the tops to the compost heap and tread back the soil loosened in the rows. The fly is attracted by the smell of carrots and likes to lay its eggs in loose soil.

Keep cauliflowers well watered with diluted liquid manure; they are the hungriest and thirstiest of plants, although celery must run them very close. Celery is naturally a ditch plant and does well in a trench with soil banked on either side. These ridges are useful for catch crops of lettuce or radish; when they have been gathered, the soil is used for successive earthing up of the celery for obtaining well-blanched stems.

Sweetcorn needs a sheltered, moist spot. Sow the seed to fill a square area rather than in rows. This assists pollination.

Peas can still be sown, but it's a good plan to leave the finished seed bed, after raking it over, at least 5 cm/2 in below the surrounding soil. You can then give them plenty of water.

In the third week, harden off tomato plants for outdoors. An improvised polythene-covered frame will suffice until the plants are put in their final positions early in June.

June

Dwarf and runner beans can be sown for a continuation of supply or if previous sowings have failed.

Lettuces will bolt if planted out in sunny positions. It is far better to sow thinly and then thin out, using any thinnings for salads. Afternoon shade provided by taller plants will lengthen the growing season.

Water will be required by most vegetables if rainfall is light; if it has been standing in tanks, so much the better. Always give a thorough watering; the effect of dribbles is to bring roots to the surface, only to be left high and dry. An all-night drenching from a sprinkler hose will do wonders to beans, lettuce, beet, celery and cauliflowers during a dry spell. In fact, plants benefit from evening soakings far more than any in the morning; the morning is a good time to add a mulch of lawn mowings before the sun can bake the surface of the soil. Mowings will gradually disappear as earth worms take them down, thus helping to aerate the soil and increase its fertility.

July

Complete planting of cabbages, savoys, Brussels sprouts, broccoli and leeks.

Swedes and hardy turnips can still be sown in the south of England or similar climates.

Spinach-beet and Swiss chard can be sown for next spring cropping.

Repeatedly pinch out side shoots from tomatoes, except bush varieties.

Harvest shallots and onions as they ripen and keep runner and dwarf beans picked as soon as they are large enough. Beans must never be allowed to grow coarse or they'll become unproductive.

Sow winter radish and thin to 15 cm/6 in apart.

A sowing of parsley in a sheltered spot should withstand the winter.

Dig early potatoes if ready. Keep the soil moist, remembering that showery weather is usually a good time to give a crop a soaking.

As plots become vacant, for example after onions have been harvested, it is a good plan to dig the soil, incorporating leafy vegetable rubbish and compost in shallow trenches as the digging proceeds across the plot. Woody waste such as cabbage stems are best disposed of on a bonfire, the plant ash being collected and kept in a dry place.

A sowing of a suitable variety of spring cabbage can be made in northern districts during the last week of July. In warmer areas, this is best deferred until the first week in August. Care in selection of a variety suitable to the district is advisable, as this is such a valuable crop.

Cucumbers, marrows and beans will benefit from good soakings of rain water that has been warmed by the sun. An excellent liquid manure can be made by chopping nettles or comfrey into rain-storage tanks and allowing them to soak for a few days. Tomatoes, in particular, benefit from this liquid, supplemented by a dressing of wood ash round the roots and followed by a mulch of lawn mowings. The plants will make rapid growth and set their trusses of fruit early.

August

The soil may now be rather dry for sowing seeds, and it's not advisable to water seeds after they are sown. You can overcome this by drawing a drill slightly deeper than normal, soaking this and sowing on top, then covering the seeds with fine sifted soil mixed with leaf mould or peat. The dry layer above the seeds will prevent rapid evaporation, keeping the seeds moist enough for quick germination. This method works well with seeds sown in August, such as onions, lettuce, winter radish and spring cabbage. If drought conditions prevail, a soaking from a fine sprinkler or a can with a fine rose can be followed with a light covering of hedge trimmings. These will soon wilt, but will prevent caking of the surface. Alternatively, you can use cloches after the watering, the cloches being lightly covered with hay or prunings for a day.

From spring until autumn, grass mowings not required for mulching should be rotted down on a compost heap. Layers of grass, not more than 5–7.5 cm/2–3 in thick, should be interspersed with garden and kitchen waste. Rotting will be faster if smaller quantities of animal manure are spread between layers and a dusting of lime is added from time to time. Good composting is quite an art, but there is no finer material obtainable for plant feeding than a well-rotted compost. Spread as a mulch between crops or on vacant plots as a weed smother. Worms will be active in the autumn, incorporating this material into the surface soil far more effectively than the gardener can ever do by digging it in.

Pick cobs of sweetcorn while still green.

Harvest onions as soon as the tops have died down.

Continue to pick tomatoes and beans as soon as they are ready. Surplus beans freeze well.

September

Plant out winter lettuce in land manured for a previous crop. On heavy soil it is advisable to plant on top of a slight ridge to avoid damping off. You can also make a further sowing of a winter-hardy variety.

Continue to lift potatoes and main-crop carrots. Store sound roots for future use. Do not leave these vegetables in the ground when they have reached their maximum growth, as slugs and other pests can do much damage.

September can be the worst month for weeds, many of which are hurrying to ripen their seeds for the autumn winds to scatter. Remove them to the compost heap where the warmth generated by lawn mowings should destroy them.

Vacant plots can be utilised by filling (but not overcrowding) them with cabbage, winter lettuce and spinach plants.

In dry spells, celery can be earthed up 5 cm/2 in at a time. The stems will then be blanched.

Use parsley as required from the seedling rows, leaving strong plants standing about 15 cm/6 in apart. Cover them with cloches if the plot is exposed to cold winds in the winter.

If your garden is exposed, or in a frost-pocket, it is as well to prepare for a slight frost towards the end of the month. The risk is greatest during clear anti-cyclonic weather when the morning sun does the damage. Polythene sheets or even newspaper draped over tomatoes and peppers will help to protect them and can be removed after an hour or so.

Gather ripened marrows for storage in a dry place.

Sow lamb's lettuce or corn salad. This is an invaluable salad which can be used during the early spring when lettuces are scarce and expensive. Cut like spinach.

October

Continue to pick tomatoes as they ripen and, if frosts are imminent, remove whole trusses of fruit to ripen in trays lined with newspaper. They will ripen in the dark providing they have warmth. The whole plants can be lifted, complete with roots, and hung in a cool greenhouse for the remaining fruits to ripen or be used green for chutney. With some care, it is possible to have ripened tomatoes until Christmas.

Dig the remainder of main-crop potatoes; they are liable to slug infestation if left in the soil. Ensure that the minute, undeveloped potatoes are removed, otherwise these can grow next year, possibly spreading disease to both tomatoes and potatoes.

Dig parsnips as required, although they will improve if frosted and can safely remain in the soil until you need them. Beetroot and carrots will not withstand hard frosts and are better stored in dry sand or peat in a cool place.

Put annual weeds on the compost heap. Put tree leaves in a separate heap as they take much longer to rot. Keep the garden tidy, removing yellowing leaves of the cabbage family and other decaying matter which only harbours slugs and other pests in the garden and is far better on the compost heap. Heavy land should be rough dug during the autumn and given a good dressing of compost. Light soil is best composted in the spring.

Spring cabbages are planted this month. If two varieties have been sown, so much the better. They should be firmly planted, closer than other cabbages, say 30 cm/12 in apart in rows 60 cm/2 ft apart. In spring, cut alternate cabbages, leaving the others to grow larger.

A final sowing of winter-hardy lettuce can be made early in the month, covering with cloches.

Celery should be earthed up during dry spells and celeriac lifted as required, the remaining roots being covered with dry soil to protect from hard frosts.

November

Clear up fallen leaves and put in a heap. Chicken netting will prevent them blowing about and the resulting leaf mould can be used at the bottom of next year's potato drills.

It is a good plan to turn semi-rotten compost, placing the outside to the middle and the middle to the outside of the new heap. When completed, give a sloping finish, dust with garden lime and cover with old matting to keep off excessive rain.

Woody waste, potato and tomato stems and diseased plants should be burnt in a slow, smother fire, if possible covered with clods. The ash and burnt soil can be sieved when cool, kept dry and used in sowing composts next spring.

Continue forking over vacant land and burning perennial weed roots. Leave the surface rough, or cover heavy land with rotted compost. A light forking is all that will then be necessary in the spring to prepare the soil for planting and sowing.

Jerusalem artichokes can be used as required and some stored in sand for use during hard frosts. Clear out all roots as they are dug. Even small pieces will grow next year and can become invasive. If you grow horseradish, the same advice applies.

On dry soils, a sowing of broad beans will repay the effort by producing a finer crop than those sown in the spring. If land is in danger of becoming too wet, the roots will rot so use cloches to help prevent this.

Corn salad or lamb's lettuce thrives in a dry, sheltered spot and is most useful in early spring salads. Sown early this month under cloches it should provide plenty of tender green stuff in April.

December

It is better to dispose of soft vegetable waste in winter by digging it into trenches during the rough digging of vacant plots than to put it on the compost heap where vermin may be a problem.

Plan ahead for the coming year, making a list of crops which bear well on your soil and ensuring that they will be planted in proper rotation. Leaf vegetables do well on soil previously used for bean crops because of the latter's nitrogenous deposits created by bacteria from nitrogen in the air. Potatoes, if well manured, provide a well-dug soil suitable for beans and peas the following year. Root crops can follow on after members of the cabbage family – give a scattering of lime before sowing; but keep lime away from land required for potatoes, otherwise the potatoes will have scabby skins.

In a four-year crop rotation of this sort, lettuce, tomatoes, celery, leeks and onions can be fitted in where they are likely to do best; but it is advisable to move onions and leeks around from year to year.

How to Use the Lunar Calendar

When you cut down elm, pine, walnut and all other timber, cut it when the Moon is waning, in the afternoon, and not under a south wind.

Cato, *On Farming*

his calendar is designed as a practical tool for the gardener and farmer, containing the key information needed on the two monthly cycles for which there is substantial evidence of their effects on gardening: the waxing and waning Moon, and the sidereal 27-day cycle. It also includes other, less well documented but potentially important information about aspects.

Readers may wish to do their own research, sowing some of their crop at an optimal time and more at a negative time to see whether there is any difference in the results. Ideally, a proper experiment requires at least a dozen rows, with equal amounts of seed sown per row on different days, and all harvested in rotation after the same length of time. Over time, one can distinguish lunar patterns from effects created by weather or other influences.

It is not always easy to co-ordinate a gardening schedule to the Moon – we all seem to be so busy these days – but with a little planning it can be achieved, hopefully with a positive effect. Of course, there will always have to be an element of judgement and compromise. For maximum yield, one aims to sow seeds at the peak times of the relevant sidereal energy cycle, yet there is no point in doing so if the ground is too wet, too dry or too cold. Use the following information as a starting point to help you tap into the cosmic influences and improve your crops.

Identifying Your Crops

All plants can be divided into one of four groups, each related to one of the four elements: Earth, Water, Air and Fire.

EARTH
ROOT PLANTS

Asparagus	Horseradish	Onion	Spring onion
Beetroot (red beet)	Jerusalem artichoke	Parsnip	(scallion)
Carrot	Leek	Potato	Swede
Garlic	Mushroom	Radish	Turnip

WATER
LEAF PLANTS

Asparagus	Celery	Fennel	Rhubarb
Basil	Chicory (Belgian	Lettuce	Sage
Bay	endive)	Mint	Sorrel
Brussels sprout	Coriander	Mustard and cress	Spinach
Cabbage	Cress	Parsley	Thyme

AIR
FLOWERING PLANTS

Artichoke	Broccoli	Elderflower
Borage	Cauliflower	Flowering plants

FIRE
FRUIT-SEED PLANTS

Apple	Broad bean	French bean	Plum
Apricot	Cherry	Gooseberry	Pumpkin
Asparagus pea	Courgette	Marrow	Runner bean
Aubergine	(zucchini)	Nectarine	Sweetcorn (corn)
(eggplant)	Cucumber	Pea	Tomato
Blackberry	Fig	Pear	Vine

When to Sow, Cultivate and Harvest

For sowing crops, observe the four-element cycle. In the calendar, these are shown as Root, Leaf, Flower and Fruit-seed days. Use the lists above to identify the day on which your crop should be sown.

If convenient, sowings are best made on the day nearest to the middle of any of the three Moon signs of the appropriate element. Prepare the soil on the same day. Avoid sowing just before the Moon moves out of a sign. Such transition times are given to the nearest hour. In Australia, one of the fathers of bio-dynamics, Alex Podolinsky, advocates sowing just as the Moon enters a new Moon-sign element, so the seed has a full two days in that quality before it changes, on the grounds that it takes that long to germinate. That view may be important in drought-prone countries.

Bio-dynamic farmers believe that any disturbance of the soil should be carried out in the same Moon-sign element in which the seed was sown. Lettuce, for example, is sown on a Leaf day, so its soil preparation as well as subsequent thinning out, weeding and so on should also be done on a Leaf day to enhance the effect.

Both experiments and experience seem to suggest that harvesting as well as sowing should be done on the relevant element days, when the weather permits. For root crops to be stored over winter, harvest on a Root day nearest to the New Moon. Fortunately, there is no hurry in harvesting root crops, so you can usually select an optimum time.

Using the Star Rhythm

If, for practical reasons, you cannot sow at the optimum times, at least try to avoid the worst times. The following diagram shows the regular wave pattern followed by the cycle of the four elements.

			Fire	Earth	Air	Water
Aries	♈	Fire				
Taurus	♉	Earth				
Gemini	♊	Air				
Cancer	♋	Water				
Leo	♌	Fire				
Virgo	♍	Earth				
Libra	♎	Air				
Scorpio	♏	Water				
Sagittarius	♐	Fire				
Capricorn	♑	Earth				
Aquarius	♒	Air				
Pisces	♓	Water				

The four-element energy cycles

Root crops, for example, should ideally be sown during Earth days for optimal yield, but if this is impossible, try to avoid planting on days at the trough in the cycle when the Moon is in the opposite element, in this case Water days. The same principle applies to other elements.

The Best Times to Plant — Moonrise and Moonset

Gardeners are familiar with the idea that the time of day at which certain operations are performed is important. As the celestial element defines the best day for planting, Moonrise or Moonset suggests the best time of day to do the work. The calendar therefore indicates the time of Moonrise and Moonset each day, an hour either side being recommended as the best time to undertake any planting, working or gardening linked to the particular element of the day. Moonrise occurs in the daytime during the waxing phase, so this time is given for these dates. In the waning phase, Moonset occurs during the day, so this time is given. Thus Moonrise just before Full Moon happens in late afternoon. On the day of Full Moon, the Moon rises as the Sun sets.

Moonrise times are given for zero degrees longitude. For any other longitude, obtain the time of rising by adding one hour per 15 degrees of longitude due west. If your position is three degrees due west, for example, add 12 minutes to the times given in the calendar. Also the Moon rises earlier due north. Readers in other latitudes can check this by watching the Moon rise and comparing the time of day to that given here.

Moonrise and Moonset are especially significant if a relevant aspect is being formed by the Moon that day, for example with the Sun or Saturn.

Laboratory research by US biologist Frank Brown has demonstrated that the greatest metabolic rate in both plants and small animals was registered at the times of Moonrise and culmination, when it reaches its highest point in the sky about six hours later. US traditions take these as the best times of day for fishing.

For effective lunar planting, seed should really begin to germinate as soon as it is sown by beginning to absorb moisture from the soil; so it is preferable, at least in warm weather, to sow seeds in the afternoon when the soil will remain moist for longer after sowing.

Planting out crops is, in general, best done in the evening so they have the night to settle in and rest, while pruning is best done in the morning so that the Sun will dry up the cut surface, thereby inhibiting bleeding. Traditionally, crops were harvested in the morning.

Grafting is generally a spring activity and pruning is one for late autumn and winter.

It is also recommended that pruning should be done on the waning Moon and grafting on the waxing Moon. Planting out should be done in the waxing Moon, if possible in the same element in which the sowings were made.

The Harmony of a Sun–Moon Trine

The calendar gives the trine (120°) angle between Sun and Moon, as happens twice a month. This is a harmonious aspect free of stress or conflict. Its moment of linking the two luminaries is a good time for many things. Like the event of Moonrise, it seems never before to have featured in a UK lunar-gardening guide: the idea came from the American book *Gardening Success with Lunar Aspects* by Adèle Barger (1976). This aspect is of particular interest for crops ruled by the Sun, for example oranges or vines.

Growing Flowers

For Flower days, the aspects between the Moon and Venus are given. A Moon–Venus energy is ideal for sowing or planting flowers, especially roses, which are ruled by Venus. The square aspects are also included, even though some might view them as unsuitable, expressing difficulty and stress. Alternatively, they could be viewed as assisting the development of structure, so it is up to you to choose.

Trees and Perennials

When working with trees or woody plants, choose a Saturn aspect for the most propitious time. The calendar gives three types of Moon–Saturn aspect each month: the opposition (180°), the trine (120°) and the sextile (60°). Growers should be mainly concerned with the Saturn aspects on Fruit-seed days, as most of their trees will be fruit-bearing. Because trees are going to last for years, there is all the more reason to identify the optimal date for planting. There may be a choice here: if planting a honeysuckle or clematis to grow up a wall, choose a Flower day, then look for either a Saturn aspect for durability or a Venus aspect for pretty flowers.

How to Read the Calendar

Each page is devoted to a single week, and each day provides all the essential information to help you make the most of your lunar gardening, indicated by various symbols. Each piece of information will be found in the same position on the daily calendars so they will soon become familiar. The calendar gives practical notes for the days to help your understanding of the aspects given, and makes suggestions on gardening activities. The notes also give the sacred Moons, such as when Easter falls or the Jewish New Year begins. Notice that the Muslim months begin a day or two after the actual New Moon, and these beginning days should be when you can first see the thin crescent of the New Moon at dusk. There's also space to record your own gardening notes.

The following symbols are used on the calendar. The key is repeated throughout the calendar along the bottom of the pages for easy reference.

Elements

These indicate the type of crop to sow on the relevant days.

 Earth – Root days

 Air – Flower days

 Water – Leaf days

 Fire – Fruit-seed days

Sidereal Signs

These show the zodiac sign relevant to the day, and the time at which the Moon moves into the next sign.

♈	Aries (Fire)	♎	Libra (Air)
♉	Taurus (Earth)	♏	Scorpio (Water)
♊	Gemini (Air)	♐	Sagittarius (Fire)
♋	Cancer (Water)	♑	Capricorn (Earth)
♌	Leo (Fire)	♒	Aquarius (Air)
♍	Virgo (Earth)	♓	Pisces (Water)

Moon Phases

Times are given next to the Moon symbols.

● New Moon ○ Full Moon

◐ Waxing Moon, first quarter ◑ Waning Moon, third quarter

Moonrise and Moonset

Although this is not part of an ephemeris, times are given for Moonrise for the waxing Moon and Moonset for the waning Moon, as these occur during the day.

☽ Moonrise ☾ Moonset

Aspects

Conjunction, opposition and square are considered negative aspects. Trine and sextile are considered positive aspects.

☌	Conjunction (0°)		Solar Eclipse (0°)
☍	Opposition (180°)		Lunar Eclipse (180°)
△	Trine (120°)	□	Square (90°)
✶	Sextile (60°)		

Specific aspects are given that relate to Saturn, Venus and the Sun.

♄ Saturn ☉ Sun

♀ Venus

Nodes

These are the points at which the Moon crosses the ecliptic.

☊   North node   ☋   South node

Apogee and Perigee

The apogee is the time at which the Moon is furthest from the Earth in its orbit, the perigee is when it is closest to the Earth.

$\mathcal{A}$ Apogee $\mathcal{P}$ Perigee

Understanding the Entries

Here are a couple of examples, showing how to read the daily entries.

| **Wednesday 24**
Sow swedes or hardy turnips. | ♑
○ 09.00
☽ 20.40 | |

This is a Root day because the Moon is in Capricorn, an Earth constellation, shown by the zodiacal glyph on the left. The Moon-quarter symbol indicates that this is a Full Moon, its time to the nearest hour noted next to the symbol. The time of Moonrise, to the nearest ten minutes, is given next to the crescent.

| **Tuesday 27** | ♓ 12.00 ♈

☾ 09.40
☾ ⚹ ♄ 18.00 | Change 12.00
 |

The transition from one zodiac sign to another, the ingress, occurs at noon. As the Moon progresses through the zodiac, so the ruling elements shift according to the same timetable, so the morning is Pisces, a Water sign giving a Leaf day, while the afternoon is Aries, a Fire sign, giving a Fruit-seed day. Moonset is at 09.40, then in the afternoon there is a Moon-Saturn sextile (60°) aspect, which is good for trees.

Checklist for Using the Calendar

Annual crops

Follow the four-element rhythms, sowing as near to the centre of the relevant sign as is convenient. The same element-sign (Root, Leaf, Flower, Fruit-seed) reappears every nine days, so if you miss the appropriate period the next may still be convenient.

Grafting and transplanting
Try to do this kind of activity under a waxing Moon.

Harvesting
Fruits picked at New Moon will store better, whereas fruits to be eaten fresh are best picked at Full Moon. Crops should be harvested in the same Moon-sign element in which they were sown if you wish to obtain seeds for next year's crop.

Perennial crops, shrubs or trees
Try to take advantage of a Saturn–Moon aspect when planting. If a tree or bush is fruit-bearing, you can also try to plant or graft it on a Fruit-seed day.

Pruning and gelding
The lunar water uptake cycle is relevant here and near Full Moon is not recommended for pruning; try to time such activity for the waning Moon.

Sowing times
Sow and plant as close to the hour of Moonrise as possible, with adjustments to your longitude and latitude. Avoid sowing for a few hours either side of the nodes, the perigee or an eclipse. Where drought is a problem, note that seeds tend to absorb the greatest amount of water on the days prior to the Full Moon, so sowing at this time should lead to optimal germination.

Times and Time Zones

All times are given in the 24-hour clock. Aspect times are given to the nearest ten minutes, Moonrise and Moonset times to the nearest ten minutes and other times to the nearest hour.

All times are GMT, or British Summer Time (BST, 1 hour added). Users in other parts of the world will need to adjust the times according to their time zone, adding or subtracting the number of hours given below.

Time Zone Adjustments for North America		Time Zone Adjustments for Australasia	
Atlantic	-4 hours	New Zealand	+12 hours
Eastern	-5 hours	Western Australia	+ 8 hours
Central	-6 hours	Southern Australia	+ 9½ hours
Mountain	-7 hours	Northern Territory	+ 9½ hours
Pacific	-8 hours	New South Wales	+ 10 hours
Yukon	-9 hours	Victoria	+ 10 hours
Alaska-Hawaii	-10 hours	Queensland	+ 10 hours
Bering	-11 hours	Tasmania	+ 10 hours

October 2017

Sunday 1

♑

☽ 17.00

♈	♉	♊	♋	♌	♍
Aries	Taurus	Gemini	Cancer	Leo	Virgo
Fire	*Earth*	*Air*	*Water*	*Fire*	*Earth*

October 2017

Monday 2

♑ 04.00 ♒

☊ 03.00

☽ 17.20

PM only

Tuesday 3

♒

☽ 17.40

Wednesday 4

♒ 11.00 ♓

☽ 18.00

Change 11.00

Thursday 5

Hunter's Moon: tonight's full moon illuminates the sky from sunset til sunrise.

♓

○ 20.00

☽ 18.20

Friday 6

Sow varieties of lettuce in the morning for over-wintering under cloches.

♓ 15.00 ♈

☾ △ ♄ 12.30

☾ 07.50

Change 15.00

Saturday 7

Pick late tomatoes and let them ripen in trays. Work on any fruit trees, especially around 10am.

♈

☾ 09.20

Sunday 8

♈ 17.00 ♉

☾ △ ♀ 14.50

☾ 10.40

Change 17.00

♎ Libra *Air*	♏ Scorpio *Water*	♐ Sagittarius *Fire*	♑ Capricorn *Earth*	♒ Aquarius *Air*	♓ Pisces *Water*

October 2017

Monday 9

♉

☾ 12.00

ℙ 06.00

PM only

Tuesday 10

♉ 19.00 ♊

☾ △ ☉ 07.10

☾ 13.10

Change 19.00

Wednesday 11

♊

☾ 14.20

Thursday 12

♊ 22.00 ♋

◐

☾ 15.00

Friday 13

Start planting winter lettuce
around 3 pm and force-grow
rhubarb in a warm greenhouse.

♋

☾ ✳ ♀ 05.00

☾ 15.40

Saturday 14

Take cuttings of bay and rue.
Divide roots of mint to re-plant
elsewhere.

♋

☊ 23.00

☾ 16.10

AM only

Sunday 15

Pick and store apples and pears
as they mature. Cut out the
fruited blackberry and loganberry
canes and train in new shoots.

♋ 02.00 ♌

☾ 16.40

| ♀ Venus | ☉ Sun | △ Trine | ♂ Conjunction | ● Solar eclipse |
| ♄ Saturn | □ Square | ✳ Sextile | ☍ Opposition | ☌ Lunar eclipse |

October 2017

Monday 16

♌

☾ 17.00

Tuesday 17

The Sun passes by Spica today, the benevolent star of the grain harvest.

♌ 08.00 ♍

☾ 17.10

Change 08.00

Wednesday 18

Dig up and store maincrop potatoes and lift and store beetroots.

♍

☾ 17.30

Thursday 19

The Indian festival of Diwali begins. Wish your family Shubh Diwali and light candles.

♍ 15.00 ♎

● 20.00

☾ 17.50

☾ ⚹ ♄ 14.20

Change 15.00

Friday 20

Lift and store summer-flowering bulbs.

♎

☽ 08.10

Saturday 21

♎

☽ 09.20

Sunday 22

Plant winter lettuce in the morning, around 10 am. Pick leafy herbs to store over winter.

♎ 01.00 ♏

☽ 10.30

● New Moon   ◐ 1st quarter   ☽ Moonrise   ☊ North node   𝒜 Apogee
○ Full Moon   ◑ 3rd quarter   ☾ Moonset   ☋ South node   𝒫 Perigee

October 2017

Monday 23
Do grafting work with trees around 11 am. Diwali ends.

♏

☽ ✳ ♀ 11.10

☽ 11.30

Tuesday 24

♏ 13.00 ♐

☽ ♂ ♄ 12.50

☽ 12.30

Change 13.00

Wednesday 25

♐

☽ ✳ ☉ 05.10

☽ 13.20

♌ 02.00

Thursday 26

♐

☽ 14.00

Friday 27

♐ 02.00 ♑

◐

☽ 14.40

Saturday 28

♑

☽ 15.00

Sunday 29
End of British Summer Time: clocks go back one hour.

♑ 12.00 ♒

�135 07.00

PM only

☽ 14.30

☽ ✳ ♄ 13.00

♈ Aries *Fire*	♉ Taurus *Earth*	♊ Gemini *Air*	♋ Cancer *Water*	♌ Leo *Fire*	♍ Virgo *Earth*

October/November 2017

Monday 30
An excellent flower day: prepare new rose beds for planting or plant lily-of-the-valley in the evening.

≈

☽ 14.50

☽ △ ☉ 13.30

Tuesday 31
Halloween, traditionally a time of otherwordly inteference in human affairs.

≈ 20.00 ♓

☽ 15.10

Change 20.00

Wednesday 1
Compost the leaves you rake up in the garden.

♓

☽ 15.20

Thursday 2

♓ 24.00 ♈

☽ 15.40

Friday 3
Work with fruit trees today, in the morning. Plant gooseberry bushes and raspberry canes, and sow round-seeded peas.

♈

☽ 16.10

Saturday 4
Enjoy a night-time walk under the November Full Moon.

♈

○ 05.00

☾ 07.10

Sunday 5
Turn over half-rotted compost and cover heavy land with rotted-down compost.

♈ 01.00 ♉

☾ 08.40

♎	♏	♐	♑	≈	♓
Libra	Scorpio	Sagittarius	Capricorn	Aquarius	Pisces
Air	Water	Fire	Earth	Air	Water

November 2017

Monday 6

♉

☽ 10.00

♇ 00.00

PM only

Tuesday 7

The pagan quarter-day of Samhain: a gathering of the clans before winter begins. A fine flower-day with both Venus and Saturn aspects.

♉ 01.00 ♊

☽ △ ♀ 10.40

☽ 11.10

Wednesday 8

♊

☽ △ ⊙ 13.30

☽ 12.00

Thursday 9

Prune trees.

♊ 03.00 ♋

☽ 12.40

Friday 10

♋

☽ 13.20

☊ 23.00

AM only

Saturday 11

♋ 06.00 ♌

☽ △ ♄ 08.50

☽ 13.40

Change 06.00

Sunday 12

♌

☽ 14.00

| ♀ Venus | ⊙ Sun | △ Trine | ♂ Conjunction | ◖ Solar eclipse |
| ♄ Saturn | ▢ Square | ✳ Sextile | ☍ Opposition | ◗ Lunar eclipse |

November 2017

Monday 13

Watch the meeting of Venus and Jupiter, the two brightest planets in the night sky.

♌ 12.00 ♍

☾ ⚹ ☉ 07.00

☾ 14.20

Change 12.00

Tuesday 14

♍

☾ 14.40

Wednesday 15

♍ 21.00 ♎

☾ 15.00

Thursday 16

Moonset near 4 pm is a time for indoor flower work.

♎

☾ 15.20

Friday 17

Plant tulips, hardy climbers and roses, as the Moon meets Venus this morning.

♎

☾ ☌ ♀ 08.20

☾ 15.40

Saturday 18

♎ 07.00 ♏

● 12.00

Change 07.00

Sunday 19

♏

☽ 08.20

● New Moon   ◐ 1st quarter   ☽ Moonrise   ☊ North node   𝒜 Apogee
○ Full Moon   ◑ 3rd quarter   ☾ Moonset   ☋ South node   𝒫 Perigee

November 2017

Monday 20

♏ 19.00 ♐

☽ 09.20

Change 19.00

Tuesday 21

♐

☽ 10.20

♓ 19.00

Wednesday 22

♐

☽ 11.00

Thursday 23

♐ 08.00 ♑

☽ 11.40

Change 08.00

Friday 24

Finish digging new beds and
borders for winter watering.

♑

☽ 12.10

Saturday 25

♑ 21.00 ♒

♉ 08.00

☽ 12.30

PM only

Sunday 26

Prick out any perennials you have
raised in the greenhouse and sow
winter bedding plants.

♒

◑

☽ 12.50

♈	♉	♊	♋	♌	♍
Aries	Taurus	Gemini	Cancer	Leo	Virgo
Fire	Earth	Air	Water	Fire	Earth

November/December 2017

Monday 27

Cut back and tidy any flowering plants in the afternoon. In the greenhouse, start forcing bulbs and sow seed of most alpines. Finish planting roses.

≈

☽ 13.10

Tuesday 28

For early risers, Venus as the Morning Star sets in the East, it will now go behind the Sun.

≈ 06.00 ♓

☽ △ ♀ 09.40

☽ 13.30

Change 06.00

Wednesday 29

Lift chicory and asparagus. Re-pot mint in the greenhouse. Take cuttings of bay and rue and place them in pots of sand.

♓

☽ △ ☉ 05.20

☽ 13.50

Thursday 30

Plant fruit trees and bushes in afternoon. Soak dry tree roots before planting and prune fruit trees after planting. Stake fruit trees. St Andrews' Day.

♓ 11.00 ♈

☽ △ ♄ 16.50

☽ 14.10

Change 11.00

Friday 1

Sow melons for an early crop and early peas and dwarf beans for cropping under glass, around 3 pm.

♈

☽ 14.30

Saturday 2

♈ 12.00 ♉

☽ 15.00

Change 12.00

Sunday 3

A 'Supermoon' (conjunct perigee). Admire how high the Full Moon rises in the night sky in the constellation of the Bull. First Sunday of Advent.

♉

○ 16.00

♎	♏	♐	♑	≈	♓
Libra	Scorpio	Sagittarius	Capricorn	Aquarius	Pisces
Air	Water	Fire	Earth	Air	Water

December 2017

Monday 4

♂ 11.00 ♊

☾ 08.40

ℙ 09.00

No Planting

✗

Tuesday 5

Pot on autumn-sown sweet peas.

♊

☾ 09.50

Wednesday 6

St Nicholas's Day

♊ 11.00 ♋

☾ 10.40

Change 11.00

Thursday 7

♋

☾ △ ♀ 09.00

☾ 11.20

Friday 8

Work on vines or other fruits in the greenhouse.

♋ 13.00 ♌

☊ 01.00

☾ 11.50

PM only

Saturday 9

Continue working with vines and fruits.

♌

☾ 12.10

Sunday 10

♌ 18.00 ♍

◗

☾ 12.30

Change 18.00

♀ Venus	⊙ Sun	△ Trine	♂ Conjunction	● Solar eclipse
♄ Saturn	□ Square	✳ Sextile	☍ Opposition	☋ Lunar eclipse

December 2017

Monday 11

♍

☾ 12.50

Tuesday 12

♍

☾ ⚹ ♀ 06.40

☾ 13.00

Wednesday 13

Work with flowering shrubs
and trees around noon. The
multi-coloured Geminids meteor
shower is the best one of the
year.

♍ 03.00 ♎

☾ ⚹ ♄ 12.30

☾ 13.20

Thursday 14

Cut down old raspberry canes.

♎

☾ 13.40

Friday 15

♎ 13.00 ♏

☾ 14.10

Change 13.00

Saturday 16

♏

☾ 14.40

Sunday 17

Dig soft vegetable waste into
trenches under the New Moon.

♏

☾ ♂ ♀ 18.30

☾ 15.20

● New Moon   ◑ 1st quarter   ☽ Moonrise   ☊ North node   𝒜 Apogee
○ Full Moon   ◐ 3rd quarter   ☾ Moonset   ☋ South node   𝒫 Perigee

December 2017

Monday 18
Work on fruit trees, around noon.

♏ 02.00 ♐
● 07.00
☽ 08.10

☽ ☌ ♄ 13.10

Tuesday 19

♐

☽ 09.00
𝒜 01.00

Wednesday 20

♐ 15.00 ♑

☽ 09.40

Change 15.00

Thursday 21
Winter Solstice, the shortest day and longest night, when the Sun crosses over the Galactic Equator just after 4 pm.

♑

☽ 10.10

Friday 22
Clear vegetable plots and dispose of soft vegetable waste by digging it into trenches.

♑

☊ 10.00

☽ 10.30

No Planting

X

Saturday 23
A fine flower day with lovely sextiles to Venus, Saturn and the Sun – ideal for a party.

♑ 03.00 ♒

☽ 11.00

☽ ✶ ♀ 10.10
☽ ✶ ♄ 15.30
☽ ✶ ☉ 19.00

Sunday 24
Plant shrubs if the weather permits, and prune back established rose beds.

♒

☽ 11.10

♈	♉	♊	♋	♌	♍
Aries	Taurus	Gemini	Cancer	Leo	Virgo
Fire	*Earth*	*Air*	*Water*	*Fire*	*Earth*

December 2017

Monday 25
Christmas Day. A meeting of Venus and Saturn in the evening favours a family re-union then.

♒ 13.00 ♓

☽ 11.30

Change 13.00

Tuesday 26
Boxing Day

♓

◑

☽ 11.50

Wednesday 27
Christmas Day (substitute day) bank holiday

♓ 20.00 ♈

☽ 12.10

Change 20.00

Thursday 28
A fine fruit-day with harmonious trines to Saturn, Venus and the Sun.

♈

☽ 12.30

☽ △ ♄ 08.00
☽ △ ♀ 13.40
☽ △ ☉ 18.50

Friday 29

♈ 23.00 ♉

☽ 13.00

Saturday 30

♉

☽ 13.30

Sunday 31
New Year's Eve (Hogmanay in Scotland)

♉ 23.00 ♊

☽ 14.20

♎	♏	♐	♑	♒	♓
Libra	Scorpio	Sagittarius	Capricorn	Aquarius	Pisces
Air	Water	Fire	Earth	Air	Water

January 2018

Monday 1

New Year's Day. Tend to indoor flowers this morning to take advantage of this flower day.

♊

☽ 15.20

℘ 22.00

AM only

Tuesday 2

A 'Supermoon' (conjunct perigee). Stay up late to see how this midwinter Full Moon rides high in the night sky.

♊ 22.00 ♋

○ 02.00

☾ 08.30

Wednesday 3

Perihelion at 6 am, as the Earth reaches its nearest point to the Sun in midwinter. Danger of floods, with Full Moon, perigee and perihelion.

♋

☾ 09.10

Thursday 4

♋ 22.00 ♌

☋ 08.00

☾ 09.40

PM only

Friday 5

Twelfth Night, the last of the Holy nights of Christmas.

♌

☾ △ ♄ 11.20

☾ 10.10

Saturday 6

Epiphany, when gifts of Gold, Frankincense and Myrrh were brought by the three Magi (astrologers) to the baby Jesus.

♌

☾ △ ♀ 10.20

☾ △ ⊙ 11.40

☾ 10.30

Sunday 7

♌ 02.00 ♍

☾ 10.50

| ♀ Venus | ⊙ Sun | △ Trine | ♂ Conjunction | ◗ Solar eclipse |
| ♄ Saturn | ☐ Square | ✶ Sextile | ☍ Opposition | ◗ Lunar eclipse |

January 2018

Monday 8

♍
◑
☽ 11.10

Tuesday 9

♍ 09.00 ♎
☽ 11.30

Change 09.00

Wednesday 10

♎
☽ 11.50

Thursday 11

A good day to work in the
greenhouse, with two beautiful
aspects in the afternoon.

♎ 19.00 ♏
☽ 12.10

☽ ⚹ ☉ 13.40
☽ ⚹ ♀ 14.50

Change 19.00

Friday 12

♏
☽ 12.40

Saturday 13

♏
☽ 13.20

Sunday 14

♏ 08.00 ♐
☽ 14.00

Change 08.00

● New Moon   ◑ 1st quarter   ☽ Moonrise   ☊ North node   ⒜ Apogee
○ Full Moon   ◐ 3rd quarter   ☾ Moonset   ☋ South node   ℗ Perigee

January 2018

Monday 15
Cut out any dead or diseased wood from fruit trees.

♐
☾ 14.50
A 02.00

Tuesday 16
Work in greenhouse with fruit crops in the afternoon.

♐ 21.00 ♑
☾ 15.50

Wednesday 17
Spread compost on empty ground.

♑
● 02.00   ☽ ♂ ♀ 06.30
☽ 08.10

Thursday 18
After the New Moon, the Calendar now switches over to give Moonrise time.

♑
☊ 14.00   No Planting
☽ 08.40

X

Friday 19

♑ 09.00 ♒
☽ 09.00

Change 09.00

Saturday 20

♒
☽ 09.20

Sunday 21

♒ 19.00 ♓
☽ 09.40

Change 19.00

♈	♉	♊	♋	♌	♍
Aries	Taurus	Gemini	Cancer	Leo	Virgo
Fire	*Earth*	*Air*	*Water*	*Fire*	*Earth*

January 2018

Monday 22

Sow salad crops in the greenhouse or in plastic cloches. Two harmonious sextiles chime today.

♓

☽ 10.00

☽ ⚹ ☉ 10.50
☽ ⚹ ♀ 17.30

Tuesday 23

If weather permits, clear dead material from leafy plants.

♓

☽ 10.20

Wednesday 24

♓ 03.00 ♈
◗
☽ 10.40

Thursday 25

Burns Night. *My love is like a red, red rose...* Enjoy some haggis to mark the occasion.

♈

☽ 11.00

Friday 26

♈ 08.00 ♉

☽ 11.30

Change 08.00

Saturday 27

Sow or tend to any root crops, around 1 pm. Work the ground ready for planting.

♉

☽ 12.10

☽ △ ☉ 05.40
☽ △ ♀ 13.30

Sunday 28

♉ 09.00 ♊

☽ 13.00

Change 09.00

 ♎ Libra *Air*
 ♏ Scorpio *Water*
 ♐ Sagittarius *Fire*
 ♑ Capricorn *Earth*
≈ Aquarius *Air*
♓ Pisces *Water*

January 2018

Monday 29

♊

☽ 14.10

Tuesday 30

It's perigee, so keep out of the garden.

♊ 09.00 ♋

☽ 15.30

♇ 10.00

No Planting

Wednesday 31

This is a Supermoon – it looks extra large – AND a Blue Moon (two in one month) AND a total Lunar eclipse, visible in Europe.

♋

☽ 13.00

☊ 19.00

No Planting

Gardening Notes

♀ Venus	☉ Sun	△ Trine	♂ Conjunction	☀ Solar eclipse
♄ Saturn	□ Square	✳ Sextile	☍ Opposition	☽ Lunar eclipse

February 2018

February Reminders

Thursday 1
Venus appears as the Evening Star.

♋ 10.00 ♌

☾ 08.10

Change 10.00

Friday 2
Candlemas, the old English quarter-day. Also Groundhog Day in America for making predictions on the arrival of spring.

♌

☾ 08.30

Saturday 3
The pagan fire-festival of Imbolc marks the first promise of spring. Enjoy a log fire.

♌ 12.00 ♍

☾ 08.50

Change 12.00

Sunday 4

♍

☾ 09.10

● New Moon   ◑ 1st quarter   ☽ Moonrise   ♌ North node   𝒜 Apogee

○ Full Moon   ◑ 3rd quarter   ☾ Moonset   ☋ South node   𝒫 Perigee

February 2018

Monday 5
♍ 17.00 ♎
☽ △ ♀ 15.30
☽ 09.30
Change 17.00

Tuesday 6
Start some early protected cauliflowers today, sowing them around 2 pm.
♎
☽ ✳ ♄ 14.10
☽ 09.50

Wednesday 7
♎
◑
☽ 10.20

Thursday 8
♎ 02.00 ♏
☽ 10.40

Friday 9
♏
☽ 11.20

Saturday 10
♏ 14.00 ♐
☽ ✳ ☉ 09.10
☽ 12.00
Change 14.00

Sunday 11
Tend fruit trees today as the Moon chimes with Saturn.
♐
☽ ☌ ♄ 14.20
☽ 12.50
♄ 14.00

♈	♉	♊	♋	♌	♍
Aries	Taurus	Gemini	Cancer	Leo	Virgo
Fire	*Earth*	*Air*	*Water*	*Fire*	*Earth*

February 2018

Monday 12

Sow early peas and beans in a south-facing sheltered area, under cloches if necessary, around Moonset at 2 pm.

♐

☾ 13.40

Tuesday 13

It's Mardi Gras, so go a bit wild. Or make pancakes, as it's also Shrove Tuesday. Prune or cut back trees.

♐ 03.00 ♑

☾ 14.40

Wednesday 14

Ash Wednesday, Lent begins: renounce something, such as eggs or cheese to help the breeding farm animals.

♑

♋ 21.00

☾ 15.50

AM only

Thursday 15

Partial Solar eclipse. Buddhist Nirvana Day.

♑ 15.00 ♒

● 21.00

☾ 17.00

No Planting

X

Friday 16

Chinese New Year of the Earth Dog. Good flower-day in the afternoon.

♒

☽ 07.30

☽ ⚹ ♄ 15.00

☽ ☌ ♀ 16.40

Saturday 17

Bring in bulbs for indoor flowering as they become ready.

♒

☽ 07.50

Sunday 18

♒ 01.00 ♓

☽ 08.00

♎	♏	♐	♑	♒	♓
Libra	Scorpio	Sagittarius	Capricorn	Aquarius	Pisces
Air	Water	Fire	Earth	Air	Water

February 2018

Monday 19

♓

☽ 08.20

Tuesday 20

♓ 09.00 ♈

☽ 08.40

Change 09.00

Wednesday 21

Work with fruit trees in early morning.

♈

☽ 09.00

☽ △ ♄ 07.10
☽ ✶ ♀ 19.20

Thursday 22

♈ 14.00 ♉

☽ 09.30

Change 14.00

Friday 23

Trim back and begin to water fuchsia and pelagonium roots to encourage them back to life.

♉

◑

☽ 10.10

Saturday 24

♉ 17.00 ♊

☽ 10.50

Change 17.00

Sunday 25

♊

☽ 11.50

☽ △ ☉ 14.40

| ♀ Venus | ☉ Sun | △ Trine | ♂ Conjunction | ● Solar eclipse |
| ♄ Saturn | □ Square | ✶ Sextile | ☍ Opposition | ◗ Lunar eclipse |

February 2018

Monday 26

♊ 19.00 ♋

☽ △ ♀ 11.10

☽ 13.00

Change 19.00

Tuesday 27

♋

☽ 14.20

𝑃 15.00

No Planting

✗

Wednesday 28

♋ 20.00 ♌

☊ 05.00

☽ 15.50

PM only

Gardening Notes

March 2018

March Reminders ————————

Thursday 1

St David's Day, the feast day of
the patron saint of Wales.

♌

☽ 17.10

☽ △ ♄ 18.10

Friday 2

You may sense the Full Moon
energies stirring in yourself, or
indeed in your garden, in days
leading up to it.

♌ 22.00 ♍

○ 01.00

☾ 07.00

Saturday 3

Sow new Jerusalem artichokes
today, keeping them a good
30 cm apart, also parsnips, garlic,
carrots or radishes.

♍

☾ 07.20

Sunday 4

♍

☾ 07.40

♈	♉	♊	♋	♌	♍
Aries	Taurus	Gemini	Cancer	Leo	Virgo
Fire	Earth	Air	Water	Fire	Earth

March 2018

Monday 5

♍ 03.00 ♎

☾ 08.00

Tuesday 6

♎

☾ △ ☉ 19.30

☾ 08.20

Wednesday 7

♎ 11.00 ♏

☾ 08.40

Change 11.00

Thursday 8

Start sowing salad crops and spinach, and some early cabbage and Brussels sprouts.

♏

☾ 09.10

Friday 9

Continue with leaf crops in the morning.

♏ 22.00 ♐

◑

☾ 09.50

Saturday 10

♐

☾ 10.40

Sunday 11

Mothering Sunday – visit the church where you were baptised or give Mum some flowers.

♐

☾ 11.30

𝒜 09.00

♎	♏	♐	♑	♒	♓
Libra	Scorpio	Sagittarius	Capricorn	Aquarius	Pisces
Air	Water	Fire	Earth	Air	Water

March 2018

Monday 12
The elements change around 11 am, from fruit-seed to root so plan your work accordingly.

⚐ 11.00 ♑

☾ 12.30

☾ ⚹ ☉ 05.40

Change 11.00

Tuesday 13
Dig over garden and spread compost.

♑

☾ 13.40

☾ ⚹ ♀ 15.20

Wednesday 14

♑ 23.00 ♒

☾ 14.40

☊ 04.00

PM only

Thursday 15

♒

☾ 15.50

Friday 16

♒

☾ 17.10

Saturday 17
St Patrick's Day

♒ 08.00 ♓

● 13.00

Change 08.00

Sunday 18
Hindu New Year

♓

☽ 06.30

| ♀ Venus | ☉ Sun | △ Trine | ♂ Conjunction | ◖ Solar eclipse |
| ♄ Saturn | □ Square | ⚹ Sextile | ☍ Opposition | ☌ Lunar eclipse |

March 2018

Monday 19

♓ 15.00 ♈

☽ 06.50

Change 15.00

Tuesday 20

Spring Equinox. It's Nouvuz, the Persian New Year. Sow or tend to fruit trees, around 4 pm.

♈

☽ △ ♄ 16.00

☽ 07.10

Wednesday 21

♈ 19.00 ♉

☽ 07.30

Change 19.00

Thursday 22

Parsnips, garlic, carrots and radishes can be sown today.

♉

☽ ⚹ ☉ 08.20

☽ 08.10

Friday 23

Continue from yesterday.

♉ 23.00 ♊

☽ ⚹ ♀ 17.10

☽ 08.50

Saturday 24

♊

◑

☽ 09.40

Sunday 25

Palm Sunday, start of Holy Week. British Summer Time begins: put your clocks forward by one hour.

♊

☽ 11.50

● New Moon	◐ 1st quarter	☽ Moonrise	☊ North node	⚸ Apogee
○ Full Moon	◑ 3rd quarter	☾ Moonset	☋ South node	⟟ Perigee

March 2018

Monday 26	♊ 03.00 ♋		No Planting
	☽ 13.10		✗
	♇ 17.00		
Tuesday 27	♋	♎ 12.00	No Planting
	☽ 14.30		✗
Wednesday 28	♋ 06.00 ♌	☽ △ ♀ 09.30	🍃
	☽ 15.50		Change 06.00
			🍊
Thursday 29	♌	☽ △ ♄ 06.30	🍊
Maundy Thursday. Plant late-flowering strawberries on suitable sites, around 4 pm. Complete this month's fruit planting today.	☽ 17.10		
Friday 30	♌ 09.00 ♍		🍊
Good Friday	☽ 18.30		Change 09.00
			🌿
Saturday 31	♍		🌿
	○ 14.00		

♈	♉	♊	♋	♌	♍
Aries	Taurus	Gemini	Cancer	Leo	Virgo
Fire	*Earth*	*Air*	*Water*	*Fire*	*Earth*

April 2018

Sunday 1

Easter Sunday, first Sunday after
the Full Moon after the Spring
Equinox: the spring day of
Resurrection.

♍ 13.00 ♎

☾ 07.00

Change 13.00

♎	♏	♐	♑	♒	♓
Libra	Scorpio	Sagittarius	Capricorn	Aquarius	Pisces
Air	*Water*	*Fire*	*Earth*	*Air*	*Water*

April 2018

Monday 2
Easter Monday. Tend to flowering bushes this afternoon.

♎︎

☾ 07.20

☾ ✳ ♄ 16.20

Tuesday 3
Plant out hardy perennials raised from seed. Dead head daffodils as the flowers fade.

♎︎ 21.00 ♏︎

☾ 07.40

Wednesday 4

♏︎

☾ 08.10

Thursday 5
Feel the harmony of the Sun–Moon trine.

♏︎

☾ 08.50

☾ △ ☉ 14.30

Friday 6

♏︎ 07.00 ♐︎

☾ 09.30

Change 07.00

Saturday 7
Plant late-flowering strawberries on suitable sites, around 1 pm.

♐︎

☾ 10.20

☾ △ ♀ 13.10

☾ ☌ ♄ 13.20

Sunday 8

♐︎ 20.00 ♑︎

◑

☾ 11.20

A 06.00

Change 20.00

| ♀ Venus | ☉ Sun | △ Trine | ☌ Conjunction | ◉ Solar eclipse |
| ♄ Saturn | □ Square | ✳ Sextile | ☍ Opposition | ◗ Lunar eclipse |

April 2018

Monday 9 Sow onion sets, maincrop carrots and globe beetroot around noon.	♑ ☾ 12.20		
Tuesday 10 Avoid gardening as the Moon meets its South node. This is a rather too drastic energy for the sensitive plant realm.	♑ ☾ 13.30	☋ 09.00	No Planting **X**
Wednesday 11	♑ 08.00 ♒ ☾ 14.40		Change 08.00
Thursday 12 A good day for setting up roses, or perennial flower bushes, around 1 pm.	♒ ☾ 15.50	☾ ✶ ♄ 13.20	
Friday 13	♒ 18.00 ♓ ☾ 17.00		Change 18.00
Saturday 14 Start some early cauliflowers (protected).	♓ ☾ 18.10		
Sunday 15	♓ 24.00 ♈ ☾ 19.30		

● New Moon   ◐ 1st quarter   ☽ Moonrise   ☊ North node   *A* Apogee

○ Full Moon   ◑ 3rd quarter   ☾ Moonset   ☋ South node   *P* Perigee

April 2018

Monday 16
Sow peas, beans or similar crops today.

♈
● 03.00
☽ 06.10

Tuesday 17
Graft during the waxing Moon.

♈
☽ 06.40

Wednesday 18
See the first crescent of the New Moon at dusk. Sow carrots in the morning.

♈ 03.00 ♉
☽ 07.10

Thursday 19
Sow root crops today, such as onion sets, maincrop carrots and globe beetroot.

♉
☽ 07.50

Friday 20

♉ 06.00 ♊
☽ ⚹ ☉ 16.20
☽ 08.40
℗ 15.00

No Planting
✗

Saturday 21
Plant out seedlings and tend to flower crops.

♊
☽ 09.40

Sunday 22
View the Lyrids meteor shower tonight. Today is Earth Day, so mull over how to save the Earth.

♊ 08.00 ♋
◑
☽ ⚹ ♀ 13.40
☽ 10.50

Change 08.00

♈	♉	♊	♋	♌	♍
Aries	Taurus	Gemini	Cancer	Leo	Virgo
Fire	Earth	Air	Water	Fire	Earth

April 2018

Monday 23
St George's Day. Shakespeare's birthday.

♋

♌ 13.00

☽ 12.10

No Planting

✗

Tuesday 24

♋ 11.00 ♌

☽ 13.30

Change 11.00

Wednesday 25
Plant out hardy perennials raised from seed.

♌

☽ △ ☉ 06.20
☽ △ ♄ 13.30

☽ 14.50

Thursday 26

♌ 16.00 ♍

☽ 16.10

Change 16.00

Friday 27
Sow root crops around 5-6 pm.

♍

☽ △ ♀ 07.50

☽ 17.30

Saturday 28
Prune out dead wood during a waning Moon.

♍ 21.00 ♎

☽ 18.40

Sunday 29

♎

☽ 20.00

♎	♏	♐	♑	♒	♓
Libra	Scorpio	Sagittarius	Capricorn	Aquarius	Pisces
Air	*Water*	*Fire*	*Earth*	*Air*	*Water*

Monday 30

Mother Nature is burgeoning in these days before April's Full Moon. How wonderful to have a Full Moon chiming with May Day.

♎

○ 02.00

☾ 05.40

Gardening Notes

♀ Venus	☉ Sun	△ Trine	☌ Conjunction	◕ Solar eclipse
♄ Saturn	□ Square	✳ Sextile	☍ Opposition	☋ Lunar eclipse

May 2018

Tuesday 1 On May Day, a May Queen honours the fertility of the Earth. Party all night, if you can.	♎ 05.00 ♏ ☾ 06.10	Change 05.00
Wednesday 2 The mating of animals will be more successful around the spring Full Moons.	♏ ☾ 06.40	☾ ☍ ♀ 10.20
Thursday 3	♏ 15.00 ♐ ☾ 07.20	Change 15.00
Friday 4 Plant out late-flowering strawberries.	♐ ☾ 08.10	
Saturday 5 The pagan spring fire-festival of Beltane to mark the start of summer; young people jump over the flames and elders drink mead.	♐ ☾ 09.10	☾ △ ☉ 08.50
Sunday 6 Draw up the soil around early potatoes.	♐ 04.00 ♑ ☾ 10.10 ⱥ 01.00	

● New Moon   ◑ 1st quarter   ☽ Moonrise   ☊ North node   ⱥ Apogee

○ Full Moon   ◐ 3rd quarter   ☾ Moonset   ☋ South node   ℘ Perigee

May 2018

Monday 7
Early May bank holiday

♑

☊ 11.00

☾ 11.10

No Planting

X

Tuesday 8

♑ 16.00 ♒
◑
☾ 12.20

Change 16.00

Wednesday 9
Prune lilac bushes after flowering.

♒

☾ 13.30

Thursday 10
A wonderful flower day, as aspects chime to Sun and Venus.

♒

☾ 14.40

☾ □ ♀ 17.40
☾ ⚹ ☉ 19.00

Friday 11
Plant out late summer cabbages and sow summer spinach.

♒ 03.00 ♓

☾ 15.50

Saturday 12
Continue from yesterday, around 5 pm.

♓

☾ 17.00

Sunday 13

♓ 09.00 ♈

☾ ⚹ ♀ 06.00

☾ 18.20

Change 09.00

♈	♉	♊	♋	♌	♍
Aries	Taurus	Gemini	Cancer	Leo	Virgo
Fire	Earth	Air	Water	Fire	Earth

May 2018

Monday 14

Water fruit trees and bushes and feed apples and pears.

♈

�}☌♄ 10.00

☽ 19.40

Tuesday 15

♈ 12.00 ♉
● 13.00

Change 12.00

Wednesday 16

The Islamic month of *Ramadan* begins, when Muslims neither eat nor drink in hours of daylight.

♉

☽ 05.40

Thursday 17

Sun meets the binary star Algol: 'Medusa's Head' is associated in skylore with a mythical monster.

♉ 13.00 ♊

☽ 06.30

ℙ 21.00

☽☌♀ 19.20

AM only

Friday 18

Sow flowers in early morning.

♊

☽ 07.30

Saturday 19

♊ 14.00 ♋

☽ 08.40

Change 14.00

Sunday 20

♋

☊ 14.00

☽ 10.00

No Planting

✗

♎	♏	♐	♑	♒	♓
Libra	Scorpio	Sagittarius	Capricorn	Aquarius	Pisces
Air	*Water*	*Fire*	*Earth*	*Air*	*Water*

May 2018

Monday 21

♋ 17.00 ♌

☽ 11.20

Change 17.00

Tuesday 22

A fine day to work with fruit-trees, especially around 5–6 pm.

♌
◐
☽ 12.40

☽ ✶ ♀ 08.50
☽ △ ♄ 17.20

Wednesday 23

Sow runner beans and set up canes to support them.

♌ 21.00 ♍

☽ 14.00

Thursday 24

Sow maincrop beetroot, swedes and turnips, and the last carrots on this root day. Relax and feel the harmonious Sun–Moon trine.

♍

☽ 15.20

☽ △ ☉ 13.50

Friday 25

♍

☽ 16.30

Saturday 26

Sow hardy and half-hardy annual flowers and plant out when all possible risk of frost has passed.

♍ 04.00 ♎

☽ 17.40

Sunday 27

Trim flower beds today, around the harmonious Moon–Venus aspect this morning.

♎

☽ 19.00

☽ ✶ ♄ 05.30
☽ △ ♀ 08.00

| ♀ Venus | ☉ Sun | △ Trine | ♂ Conjunction | ● Solar eclipse |
| ♄ Saturn | □ Square | ✶ Sextile | ☍ Opposition | ☾ Lunar eclipse |

May 2018

Monday 28
Spring bank holiday

♎ 12.00 ♏

☽ 20.10

Change 12.00

Tuesday 29

♏
○ 15.00

Wednesday 30
Sow spinach and cabbage this morning.

♏ 23.00 ♐

☾ 05.20

Thursday 31
The Sun meets the mighty rose-pink star Aldebaran, the 'Bulls-Eye', bringing good fortune.

♐

☾ 06.00

Gardening Notes

● New Moon   ◑ 1st quarter   ☽ Moonrise   ☊ North node   𝒜 Apogee

○ Full Moon   ◐ 3rd quarter   ☾ Moonset   ☋ South node   𝒫 Perigee

June 2018

June Reminders

Friday 1 Continue to sow dwarf and runner beans.	♐ ☽ 07.00	☽ ☍ ♀ 18.00	
Saturday 2	♐ 11.00 ♑ ☽ 08.00 ♃ 17.00		Change 11.00
Sunday 3	♑ ☽ 09.00	♉ 14.00	No Planting ✗

♈	♉	♊	♋	♌	♍
Aries *Fire*	Taurus *Earth*	Gemini *Air*	Cancer *Water*	Leo *Fire*	Virgo *Earth*

June 2018

Monday 4

♑

☾ 10.10

Tuesday 5

♑ 00.00 ♒

☾ 11.10

Wednesday 6

Sow hardy wild flowers, and sow wallflowers, around noon. Hoe for weeds.

♒

◑

☾ 12.20

Thursday 7

♒ 11.00 ♓

☾ △ ♀ 07.30

☾ 13.30

Change 11.00

Friday 8

Pick out shoots on aromatics such as rosemary to encourage growth.

♓

☾ 14.40

Saturday 9

♓ 19.00 ♈

☾ ⚹ ☉ 08.30

☾ 16.00

Change 19.00

Sunday 10

Tend to fruit-trees this afternoon, around 5–6 pm.

♈

☾ △ ♄ 17.20

☾ 17.20

♎	♏	♐	♑	♒	♓
Libra	Scorpio	Sagittarius	Capricorn	Aquarius	Pisces
Air	*Water*	*Fire*	*Earth*	*Air*	*Water*

June 2018

Monday 11
See the last sliver of the dying old Moon after sunset.

♈ 22.00 ♉

☾ 18.40

Tuesday 12

♉

☾ 20.00

Wednesday 13

♉ 23.00 ♊
● 21.00

Thursday 14
The Islamic month of *Ramadan* ends.

♊

☽ 05.10

P 24.00

AM only

Friday 15
Plant Brussels sprouts, as well as savoys and purple-sprouting broccoli, also spring-headed broccoli.

♊ 23.00 ♋

☽ 06.20

Saturday 16

♋

☽ 07.40

☽ ♂ ♀ 13.10

☊ 19.00

AM only

Sunday 17

♋ 24.00 ♌

☽ 09.00

♀ Venus	☉ Sun	△ Trine	♂ Conjunction	● Solar eclipse
♄ Saturn	□ Square	✳ Sextile	☍ Opposition	☽ Lunar eclipse

June 2018

Monday 18

Tend to fruit-trees in the morning, around 10–11 am.

♌

☽ 10.30

Tuesday 19

Same as yesterday, using the Moonrise hour.

♌

☽ 11.50

Wednesday 20

Take softwood cuttings of shrubs to make new plants.

♌ 03.00 ♍

◑

☽ 13.00

Thursday 21

The longest day, with Summer Solstice at 11 am BST: celebrate with friends.

♍

☽ 14.20

Friday 22

♍ 09.00 ♎

☽ 15.30

Change 09.00

Saturday 23

Midsummer's Eve, St John's Eve. A fine day for flower crops, especially woody perennials.

♎

☽ 16.50

☽ ✳ ♄ 07.50
☽ □ ♀ 17.30

Sunday 24

St John's Day. Has the St John's Wort plant come into blossom?

♎ 18.00 ♏

☽ 18.00

Change 18.00

● New Moon ◐ 1st quarter ☽ Moonrise ☊ North node 𝒜 Apogee
○ Full Moon ◑ 3rd quarter ☾ Moonset ☋ South node 𝒫 Perigee

June 2018

Monday 25

♏

☽ 19.00

Tuesday 26

♏

☽ △ ♀ 09.50

☽ 20.10

Wednesday 27

Saturn is brightest in the night sky. Enjoy an outdoor dinner, seeing the Full Moon rise as the Sun sets.

♏ 05.00 ♐

☽ 21.00

Change 05.00

Thursday 28

Saturn is brightest in the night sky. Stay up late to see how low the Full Moon is in the night sky, compared to winter-time.

♐

○ 06.00

Friday 29

The days around this June Full Moon are a fine time for the mating of animals, they are extra fertile.

♐ 18.00 ♑

☾ 05.50

Change 18.00

Saturday 30

♑

☋ 18.00

☾ 06.50

𝒜 03.00

AM only

♈	♉	♊	♋	♌	♍
Aries	Taurus	Gemini	Cancer	Leo	Virgo
Fire	Earth	Air	Water	Fire	Earth

July 2018

July Reminders —————————————

Sunday 1   ♑

♌ 08.00

♎	♏	♐	♑	♒	♓
Libra	Scorpio	Sagittarius	Capricorn	Aquarius	Pisces
Air	*Water*	*Fire*	*Earth*	*Air*	*Water*

July 2018

Monday 2

♑ 07.00 ♒

☾ 09.00

Change 07.00

Tuesday 3

Sow flowering plants around 6 pm. The harmony of this Sun–Moon trine in late afternoon, means that everyone can relax.

♒

☾ 10.10

☾ ⚹ ♄ 05.30
☾ △ ☉ 18.00

Wednesday 4

♒ 18.00 ♓

☾ 11.20

Change 18.00

Thursday 5

♓

☾ 12.30

Friday 6

Aphelion at 6 pm, when the Earth is at its furthest point from the Sun.

♓

◑

☾ 13.40

Saturday 7

Prune apple and pear trees today, during the waning Moon.

♓ 03.00 ♈

☾ 14.50

☾ △ ♀ 08.10

Sunday 8

Tend to fruit crops late afternoon.

♈

☾ 16.10

☾ ⚹ ☉ 19.00

| ♀ Venus | ☉ Sun | △ Trine | ♂ Conjunction | Solar eclipse |
| ♄ Saturn | □ Square | ⚹ Sextile | ☍ Opposition | Lunar eclipse |

July 2018

Monday 9

♈ 08.00 ♉

☾ 17.30

Change 08.00

Tuesday 10

A final earthing-up of maincrop potatoes and Jerusalem artichokes would be well favoured today.

♉

☾ 18.50

Wednesday 11

♉ 10.00 ♊

☾ 20.00

Change 10.00

Thursday 12

♊

☾ 20.50

Friday 13

Partial Solar eclipse

♊ 09.00 ♋

● 04.00

☽ 05.10

℗ 09.00

No Planting

✗

Saturday 14

♋

☊ 04.00

☽ 06.30

PM only

Sunday 15

♋ 09.00 ♌

☽ 08.00

Change 09.00

● New Moon   ◐ 1st quarter   ☽ Moonrise   ☊ North node   ℀ Apogee

○ Full Moon   ◑ 3rd quarter   ☾ Moonset   ☋ South node   ℗ Perigee

July 2018

Monday 16

Take cuttings and propagate during the waxing Moon. Work on fruit-trees around 10 am.

♌

☽ 09.30

☽ ♂ ♀ 05.40

Tuesday 17

♌ 11.00 ♍

☽ 10.50

☽ ✶ ☉ 11.50

Change 11.00

Wednesday 18

Sow turnips for winter use. Earth-up Jerusalem artichokes and maincrop potatoes.

♍

☽ 12.10

Thursday 19

♍ 15.00 ♎

◑

☽ 13.20

Change 15.00

Friday 20

Sow or transplant flowers, especially around 10 am. Lift and divide hellebores in a moist, shady spot.

♎

☽ 14.40

☽ ✶ ♄ 10.00

Saturday 21

♎ 24.00 ♏

☽ 15.50

Sunday 22

Enjoy the harmony of this Sun–Moon trine in the morning.

♏

☽ 17.00

☽ △ ☉ 10.20

♈	♉	♊	♋	♌	♍
Aries	Taurus	Gemini	Cancer	Leo	Virgo
Fire	*Earth*	*Air*	*Water*	*Fire*	*Earth*

July 2018

Monday 23

♏

☽ 18.00

Tuesday 24

♏ 11.00 ♐

☽ 18.50

Change 11.00

Wednesday 25

♐

☽ ☌ ♄ 06.50

☽ 19.40

Thursday 26

♐ 24.00 ♑

See how low this summertime Full Moon hangs in the sky! Horses are most fertile around the spring and summer Full Moons.

☽ △ ♀ 11.00

☽ 20.20

Friday 27

♑

Total Lunar eclipse, visible in Europe. Stay out of the garden. Mars would be brightest in night sky, but the Full Moon steals the show.

● 21.00

☊ 24.00

☽ 20.50

𝒜 06.00

No Planting

X

Saturday 28

♑

Sow winter radish and dig up early potatoes if they are ready. Have dinner outdoors to enjoy this summer Full Moon.

☾ 05.50

Sunday 29

♑ 13.00 ♒

Change 13.00

☾ 06.50

♎	♏	♐	♑	♒	♓
Libra	Scorpio	Sagittarius	Capricorn	Aquarius	Pisces
Air	Water	Fire	Earth	Air	Water

July 2018

Monday 30

Work on perennial flower crops in the morning. Prune apple and pear trees, and thin early dessert apples.

≈

☾ 08.00

☾ ✷ ♄ 07.50

Tuesday 31

≈

☾ 09.10

Gardening Notes

August 2018

Wednesday 1

Sow lettuce and greens for winter, leeks, late Brussels sprouts, winter cabbage, and sprouting and spring broccoli.

♒ 00.00 ♓

☾ 10.20

Thursday 2

Continue sowing from yesterday, over the morning Sun–Moon trine aspect if possible.

♓

☾ △ ☉ 07.00

☾ 11.30

Friday 3

♓ 10.00 ♈

☾ 12.40

Change 10.00

Saturday 4

♈

◑

☾ 13.50

Sunday 5

♈ 16.00 ♉

☾ 15.10

Change 16.00

● New Moon	◐ 1st quarter	☽ Moonrise	☊ North node	♉ Apogee
○ Full Moon	◑ 3rd quarter	☾ Moonset	☋ South node	℗ Perigee

August 2018

Monday 6

♉

☾ 16.30

Tuesday 7

Today is Lammas, the old English festival to mark the wheat harvest. Mark the occasion with a barbecue.

♉ 19.00 ♊

☾ 17.40

Change 19.00

Wednesday 8

Sow wallflowers and sweet Williams for next year and set out seedlings of biennials.

♊

☾ 18.40

☾ □ ♀ 07.10

Thursday 9

♊ 20.00 ♋

☾ 19.30

Change 20.00

Friday 10

Crops harvested at New Moon will keep best: do this in the morning.

♋

☾ 20.10

𝑃 18.00

☾ ⚹ ♀ 10.50

☊ 15.00

No Planting

X

Saturday 11

Partial Solar eclipse

♋ 20.00 ♌

● 11.00

No Planting

X

Sunday 12

The Perseids meteor shower, coming from the Perseus constellation, is visible after midnight.

♌

☽ 06.50

☽ △ ♄ 09.50

♈	♉	♊	♋	♌	♍
Aries	Taurus	Gemini	Cancer	Leo	Virgo
Fire	*Earth*	*Air*	*Water*	*Fire*	*Earth*

August 2018

Monday 13	♌ 20.00 ♍		
	☽ 08.20		Change 20.00

Tuesday 14
Sow root crops in late afternoon, as Venus meets the Moon.

♍

☽ ♂ ♀ 19.10

☽ 09.40

Wednesday 15

♍ 23.00 ♎

☽ 11.00

Thursday 16
Transplant flower seedlings during waxing Moon. Plant daffodils and take cuttings from rambling roses.

♎

☽ ✶ ♄ 15.10

☽ 12.20

Friday 17
Venus is highest as Evening Star.

♎

☽ 13.30

Saturday 18

♎ 06.00 ♏

◗

☽ 14.50

Change 06.00

Sunday 19
Sow winter spinach, spring cabbage and hardy lettuce today.

♏

☽ ✶ ♀ 18.10

☽ 15.50

♎	♏	♐	♑	♒	♓
Libra	Scorpio	Sagittarius	Capricorn	Aquarius	Pisces
Air	Water	Fire	Earth	Air	Water

August 2018

Monday 20

♏ 17.00 ♐

☽ 16.50

Change 17.00

Tuesday 21

A good morning to prepare the ground for planting new fruit stocks, and complete the planting of strawberry runners.

♐

☽ ☌ ♄ 10.30

☽ 17.40

Wednesday 22

Prune the fruited shoots of peach and plum trees.

♐

☽ 18.20

Thursday 23

The Sun meets Regulus, for millenia the brightest star in the constellation Leo; it moved on into Virgo recently, the sign for ecology and mindfulness.

♐ 06.00 ♑

☽ 18.50

A 11.00

Change 06.00

Friday 24

♑

☊ 06.00

☽ 19.20

PM only

Saturday 25

♑ 19.00 ♒

☽ △ ♀ 05.40

☽ 19.40

Change 19.00

Sunday 26

♒

○ 13.00

☾ ✶ ♄ 11.50

| ♀ Venus | ☉ Sun | △ Trine | ☌ Conjunction | ◖ Solar eclipse |
| ♄ Saturn | □ Square | ✶ Sextile | ☍ Opposition | ◗ Lunar eclipse |

August 2018

Monday 27
Summer bank holiday

≈

☾ 07.00

Tuesday 28

≈ 06.00 ♓

☾ 08.10

Change 06.00

Wednesday 29

♓

☾ 09.20

Thursday 30

♓ 16.00 ♈

☾☍♀ 12.00

☾ 10.30

Change 16.00

Friday 31
Sow herbs or seed crops over one
of these trine aspects.

♈

☾△♄ 07.20

☾ 11.40

☾△☉ 17.40

Gardening Notes

September 2018

September Reminders

| Saturday 1 | | ♈ 23.00 ♉ |
| | | ☾ 13.00 |

| Sunday 2 | | ♉ |
| Water your garden around 2 pm. | | ☾ 14.10 |

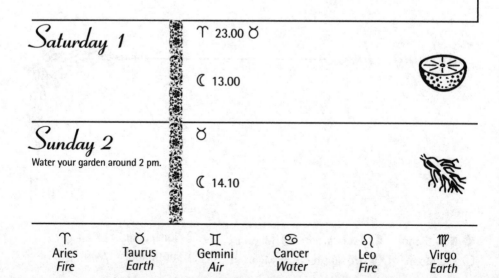

♈	♉	♊	♋	♌	♍
Aries	Taurus	Gemini	Cancer	Leo	Virgo
Fire	Earth	Air	Water	Fire	Earth

September 2018

Monday 3

♉

◐

☾ 15.20

Tuesday 4

Sow flowers in early morning.

♉ 03.00 ♊

☾ △ ♀ 06.30

☾ 16.30

Wednesday 5

♊

☾ ✶ ☉ 10.30

☾ 17.20

Thursday 6

♊ 05.00 ♋

AM only

☊ 24.00

☾ 18.00

☾ □ ♀ 11.20

Friday 7

See the fading crescent of the old Moon at dusk. Prune evergreen hedges this month. Harvest herbs for storage.

♋

☾ 18.30

Saturday 8

Pick early apples and pears while slightly under-ripe. Farmers, harvest the golden grain, for best storage, at this New Moon.

♋ 06.00 ♌

PM only

☾ ✶ ♀ 14.30

☾ 19.00

☾ △ ♄ 19.40

℘ 01.00

Sunday 9

Jewish New Year. Re-pot tomatoes sown in June. Prepare ground for planting new fruit stocks. Complete planting of strawberry runners.

♌

● 19.00

♎	♏	♐	♑	♒	♓
Libra	Scorpio	Sagittarius	Capricorn	Aquarius	Pisces
Air	Water	Fire	Earth	Air	Water

September 2018

Monday 10	♌ 07.00 ♍		Change 07.00
	☽ 07.10		
Tuesday 11	♍		
	☽ 08.30		
Wednesday 12 Islamic New Year	♍ 09.00 ♎		Change 09.00
	☽ 10.00		
Thursday 13 Transplant flower seedlings, plant daffodils and take cuttings from rambler roses, around 11 am.	♎		
	☽ 11.10		
Friday 14 Continue transplanting of flower seedlings, around 9–10 am.	♎ 15.00 ♏	☽ ✶ ☉ 09.50	Change 15.00
	☽ 12.30		
Saturday 15 Take cuttings of cherry, laurel and privet. Prepare sites for new lawns and sow seeds around 2 pm.	♏		
	☽ 13.40		
Sunday 16	♏		
	☽ 14.40		

♀ Venus	☉ Sun	△ Trine	♂ Conjunction	◐ Solar eclipse
♄ Saturn	□ Square	✶ Sextile	☍ Opposition	☽ Lunar eclipse

September 2018

Monday 17
Tend to fruit trees, with any cuttings and transplants needed.

♏ 00.00 ♐
◑
☽ 15.30

☽ ☌ ♄ 17.20

Tuesday 18

♐

☽ 16.20

Wednesday 19

♐ 13.00 ♑

☽ 16.50

☽ △ ☉ 18.10

Change 13.00

Thursday 20

♑

☽ 17.20

𝒜 01.00

☋ 11.00

No Planting

✕

Friday 21

♑

☽ 17.50

Saturday 22
Tend to perennial flower crops in late afternoon.

♑ 02.00 ♒

☽ 18.10

☽ ✳ ♄ 19.00

Sunday 23
Autumn Equinox

♒

☽ 18.20

☽ △ ♀ 05.20

● New Moon   ◑ 1st quarter   ☽ Moonrise   ☊ North node   𝒜 Apogee
○ Full Moon   ◐ 3rd quarter   ☾ Moonset   ☋ South node   𝒫 Perigee

September 2018

Monday 24

♒ 13.00 ♓

☽ 18.40

Change 13.00

Tuesday 25

The Harvest Moon stays yellow, big and low near the horizon, giving farmers that extra hour to finish their harvest.

♓

○ 04.00

☾ 07.10

Wednesday 26

Venus is now brightest as Evening Star.

♓ 21.00 ♈

☾ 08.20

Thursday 27

Use the Moonset hour for harvesting crops for sale or for consumption, but not for storage.

♈

☾ △ ♄ 13.30

☾ 09.30

Friday 28

Pick late tomatoes and let them ripen in trays. Work on any fruit trees, especially between 10–12 am.

♈

☾ 10.50

Saturday 29

Michaelmas Day

♈ 04.00 ♉

☾ 12.00

Sunday 30

Harvest Festival is celebrated this Sunday.

♉

☾ 13.10

♈	♉	♊	♋	♌	♍
Aries	Taurus	Gemini	Cancer	Leo	Virgo
Fire	Earth	Air	Water	Fire	Earth

October 2018

Monday 1	♉ 09.00 ♊ ☾ 14.20		Change 09.00
Tuesday 2	♊ ◑ ☾ 15.20	☾ △ ♀ 13.20	
Wednesday 3	♊ 12.00 ♋ ☾ 16.00		Change 12.00
Thursday 4 Plant winter lettuce in the afternoon. Force-grow rhubarb in a warm greenhouse.	♋ ☾ 16.30	☊ 04.00 ☾ ✶ ☉ 17.20	PM only
Friday 5	♋ 15.00 ♌ ☾ 17.00 P 23.00		AM only
Saturday 6 Pick and store apples and pears as they mature. Cut out the fruited blackberry and loganberry canes and train in new shoots.	♌ ☾ 17.30	☾ △ ♄ 05.40 ☾ ✶ ♀ 18.20	
Sunday 7	♌ 16.00 ♍ ☾ 17.50		Change 16.00

♎	♏	♐	♑	♒	♓
Libra *Air*	Scorpio *Water*	Sagittarius *Fire*	Capricorn *Earth*	Aquarius *Air*	Pisces *Water*

October 2018

| Monday 8 | ♍ | |
| | ☾ 18.10 | |

Tuesday 9	♍ 19.00 ♎	
	● 05.00	Change 19.00
	☽ 07.30	

Wednesday 10
Graft fruit trees and cut out
fruited blackberry and loganberry
trees.

♎

☽ ✶ ♄ 11.10

☽ 08.50

Thursday 11
Prepare new rose beds for
planting or plant lily of the
valley. Plant out herbaceous
perennials.

♎

☽ 10.10

| Friday 12 | ♎ 00.00 ♏ | |
| | ☽ 11.20 | |

| Saturday 13 | ♏ | |
| | ☽ 12.30 | |

| Sunday 14 | ♏ 09.00 ♐ | |
| | ☽ 13.30 | Change 19.00 |

| ♀ Venus | ⊙ Sun | △ Trine | ♂ Conjunction | ● Solar eclipse |
| ♄ Saturn | □ Square | ✶ Sextile | ☍ Opposition | ☾ Lunar eclipse |

October 2018

Monday 15

Pick late tomatoes and let them ripen in trays. Work on any fruit trees especially around 2 pm.

♐

☽ 14.10

☽ ⚹ ♀ 14.00

Tuesday 16

♐ 21.00 ♑

◑

☽ 14.50

Wednesday 17

The Sun passes by Spica today, the benevolent star of the grain harvest.

♑

☊ 13.00

☽ 15.20

𝒜 19.00

No Planting

✗

Thursday 18

Dig up maincrop potatoes and lift and store beetroot.

♑

☽ 15.50

Friday 19

♑ 10.00 ♒

☽ △ ☉ 13.30

☽ 16.10

Change 10.00

Saturday 20

Venus vanishes from view as the Evening Star. Tend to indoor flowers in the morning.

♒

☽ ⚹ ♄ 05.30

☽ 16.30

☽ △ ♀ 10.40

Sunday 21

♒ 21.00 ♓

☽ 16.50

● New Moon	◑ 1st quarter	☽ Moonrise	☊ North node	𝒜 Apogee
○ Full Moon	◐ 3rd quarter	☾ Moonset	☋ South node	𝒫 Perigee

October 2018

Monday 22
♓

☽ 17.00

Tuesday 23
♓

Plant herbaceous perennials and deciduous trees, but avoid frosty conditions.

☽ 17.20

Wednesday 24
♓ 05.00 ♈

Hunter's Moon: tonight's Full Moon illuminates the sky from sunset till sunrise.

○ 18.00

☽ 17.40

Change 05.00

Thursday 25
♈

☾ 08.30

Friday 26
♈ 10.00 ♉

☾ 09.50

Change 10.00

Saturday 27
♉

☾ 11.00

Sunday 28
♉ 13.00 ♊

End of British Summer Time: clocks go back one hour.

☾ 11.10

Change 13.00

♈	♉	♊	♋	♌	♍
Aries	Taurus	Gemini	Cancer	Leo	Virgo
Fire	Earth	Air	Water	Fire	Earth

October/November 2018

Monday 29	♊ ☾ 12.10	☾ △ ☉ 09.30

Tuesday 30
♊ 17.00 ♋

☾ 13.00

Change 17.00

Wednesday 31
Halloween, traditionally a time of otherwordly interference in human affairs.

♋
◐
☾ 13.40
𝄢 20.00

☊ 04.00

AM only

Thursday 1
♋ 20.00 ♌

☾ 14.10

Change 20.00

Friday 2
Use the Saturn aspect to plant gooseberry bushes and raspberry canes; sow round-seeded peas and prune trees.

♌

☾ 14.30

☾ △ ♄ 14.30

Saturday 3
♌ 23.00 ♍

☾ 14.50

Sunday 4
♍

☾ 15.10

♎	♏	♐	♑	♒	♓
Libra	Scorpio	Sagittarius	Capricorn	Aquarius	Pisces
Air	*Water*	*Fire*	*Earth*	*Air*	*Water*

November 2018

Monday 5

Venus appears as Morning Star and leads the way for the rising Sun.

♍

☾ 15.30

Tuesday 6

Cut back and tidy any flowering plants in the afternoon. In the greenhouse, start forcing bulbs and sow seed of most alpines.

♍ 03.00 ♎

☾ 15.50

☾ ☌ ♀ 08.20

Wednesday 7

The pagan quarter-day of Samhain: a gathering of the clans before winter begins. The Indian festival of *Diwali* begins.

♎

● 16.00

Thursday 8

♎ 08.00 ♏

☽ 08.00

Change 08.00

Friday 9

♏

☽ 09.10

Saturday 10

♏ 16.00 ♐

☽ 10.10

☽ ⚹ ♀ 19.50

Change 16.00

Sunday 11

Diwali ends.

♐

☽ 11.10

☽ ☌ ♄ 15.20

♀ Venus   ☉ Sun   △ Trine   ☌ Conjunction   ● Solar eclipse

♄ Saturn   □ Square   ⚹ Sextile   ☍ Opposition   ☾ Lunar eclipse

November 2018

Monday 12	♐ ☽ 11.50		
Tuesday 13	♐ 04.00 ♑ ☊ 14.00 ☽ 12.20		No Planting ✗
Wednesday 14	♑ ☽ 12.50 *A* 16.00		
Thursday 15	♑ 17.00 ♒ ◑ ☽ 13.10	☽ △ ♀ 19.10	Change 17.00
Friday 16 Finish planting roses.	♒ ☽ 13.30	☽ ✶ ♄ 17.30	
Saturday 17 Prick out any perennials you have raised in the greenhouse and sow winter bedding plants.	♒ ☽ 13.50		
Sunday 18	♒ 05.00 ♓ ☽ 14.10	☽ △ ☉ 08.00	Change 05.00

● New Moon	◑ 1st quarter	☽ Moonrise	☊ North node	*A* Apogee
○ Full Moon	◐ 3rd quarter	☾ Moonset	☋ South node	*P* Perigee

November 2018

Monday 19

Use the Moonrise hour to lift chicory and asparagus.

♓

☽ 14.30

Tuesday 20

♓ 13.00 ♈

☽ ☍ ♀ 15.40

☽ 14.50

Change 13.00

Wednesday 21

Sow fruit crops in greenhouse for next year, around 11–12 am.

♈

☽ △ ♄ 11.50

☽ 15.10

Thursday 22

♈ 18.00 ♉

☽ 15.40

Change 18.00

Friday 23

♉

○ 06.00

☾ 07.40

Saturday 24

♉ 21.00 ♊

☾ 09.00

Sunday 25

♊

☾ 10.00

♈	♉	♊	♋	♌	♍
Aries	Taurus	Gemini	Cancer	Leo	Virgo
Fire	Earth	Air	Water	Fire	Earth

November/December 2018

Monday 26

♊ 23.00 ♋

☽ 11.00

℗ 12.00

No Planting

✕

Tuesday 27

♋

♌ 05.00

☽ 11.40

☽ △ ☉ 17.40

PM only

Wednesday 28

Clear fallen leaves away from small plants so they are not too damp.

♋

☽ 12.10

Thursday 29

Plant fruit trees and bushes, soaking dry tree roots before planting, and prune fruit trees after planting. Stake trees.

♋ 01.00 ♌

☽ ✳ ♀ 08.20

☽ 12.40

Friday 30

Venus is at her brightest as the Morning Star now. St Andrew's Day, a national holiday in Scotland.

♌

◑

☽ 13.00

Saturday 1

Finish digging new beds and borders for winter weathering.

♌ 05.00 ♍

☽ 13.20

Change 05.00

Sunday 2

Advent Sunday; Christmas decorations can go up now.

♍

☽ ✳ ☉ 08.30

☽ 13.40

| ♎ Libra *Air* | ♏ Scorpio *Water* | ♐ Sagittarius *Fire* | ♑ Capricorn *Earth* | ♒ Aquarius *Air* | ♓ Pisces *Water* |

December 2018

Monday 3

♍ 09.00 ♎

☾ 14.00

Change 09.00

Tuesday 4

Moonset at 2 pm is a time for indoor flower work. Also plant tulips, hardy climbers and roses.

♎

☾ 14.20

☾ ⚹ ♄ 10.40

Wednesday 5

♎ 16.00 ♏

☾ 14.50

Change 16.00

Thursday 6

Compost the leaves you rake up in the garden. St Nicholas's Day.

♏

☾ 15.20

Friday 7

Take cuttings of bay and rue and place in pots of sand. Re-pot mint in the greenhouse.

♏

● 07.00

☽ 08.00

Saturday 8

Tend to fruit crops in the greenhouse, late afternoon.

♏ 01.00 ♐

☽ 09.00

☽ ⚹ ♀ 19.20

Sunday 9

♐

☽ 09.50

☽ ☌ ♄ 05.10

| ♀ Venus | ☉ Sun | △ Trine | ☌ Conjunction | ◑ Solar eclipse |
| ♄ Saturn | □ Square | ⚹ Sextile | ☍ Opposition | ☽ Lunar eclipse |

December 2018

Monday 10

♐ 12.00 ♑

☋ 18.00

AM only

☽ 10.20

Tuesday 11

Trim growth of globe artichokes, draw soil around the roots. Turn over half-rotted compost, cover heavy land with rotted-down compost.

♑

☽ 10.50

Wednesday 12

Continue from yesterday, digging in compost. A fine Sun–Moon aspect this afternoon.

♑

☽ ✶ ☉ 17.40

☽ 11.20

⚇ 12.00

Thursday 13

♑ 01.00 ♒

☽ 11.40

Friday 14

Finish planting roses and prune back established rose beds. Plant shrubs if the weather permits.

♒

☽ ✶ ♄ 07.30

☽ 12.00

Saturday 15

♒ 13.00 ♓

◑

☽ 12.10

Change 13.00

Sunday 16

♓

☽ 12.30

● New Moon	◑ 1st quarter	☽ Moonrise	☊ North node	⚇ Apogee
○ Full Moon	◐ 3rd quarter	☾ Moonset	☋ South node	℗ Perigee

December 2018

Monday 17
Trim back lawn edges to make the garden tidy.

♓ 23.00 ♈

☽ 12.50

Tuesday 18
Work on vines or other fruits in the greenhouse.

♈

☽ 13.10

Wednesday 19
Sow melons around 1–2 pm for an early crop, and tomatoes for a summer crop in the greenhouse. Set any fruit trees.

♈

☽ ☍ ♀ 06.50

☽ 13.30

Thursday 20
Examine stored vegetables and remove any that are diseased. Dig over the ground.

♈ 04.00 ♉

☽ 14.00

Friday 21
Winter Solstice, longest night, when the Sun crosses over the Galactic Equator just after 10 pm.

♉

☽ 14.50

Saturday 22

♉ 07.00 ♊

○ 18.00

☽ 15.40

Change 07.00

Sunday 23

♊

☾ △ ♀ 18.00

☾ 08.50

♈	♉	♊	♋	♌	♍
Aries	Taurus	Gemini	Cancer	Leo	Virgo
Fire	Earth	Air	Water	Fire	Earth

December 2018

Monday 24

Ⅱ 07.00 ♋

♌ 12.00

☽ 09.30

♇ 10.00

No Planting

✕

Tuesday 25

Christmas Day, and the Twelve Holy Nights begin.

♋

☽ 10.10

Wednesday 26

Boxing Day

♋ 08.00 ♌

☽ 10.40

Change 08.00

Thursday 27

Tend to fruit crops in greenhouse.

♌

☽ △ ♄ 11.50

☽ 11.00

Friday 28

♌ 10.00 ♍

☽ 11.20

Change 10.00

Saturday 29

♍

◑

☽ 11.40

Sunday 30

♍ 15.00 ♎

☽ 12.00

Change 15.00

♎	♏	♐	♑	♒	♓
Libra	Scorpio	Sagittarius	Capricorn	Aquarius	Pisces
Air	Water	Fire	Earth	Air	Water

December 2018

Monday 31
New Year's Eve (Hogmanay in Scotland)

♎︎

☽ 12.30

☽ ✶ ☉ 19.50

Gardening Notes

The Seasons of 2018

Young Spring was there, his head encircled with a flowery garland, and Summer, lightly clad, crowned with a wreath of corn ears; Autumn too, stained purple with treading out the vintage, and icy Winter, with white and shaggy locks.

Ovid

A highlight early this year is Venus appearing as the bright Evening Star in February, growing in brightness. Perihelion comes on 3 January, this is the time when Earth is at its nearest point to the Sun and this occurs in midwinter – a deep paradox, and a good time for the clinking of glasses and to recover from the stresses of Christmas. January has two extra-large 'Supermoon' Full Moons this year, which come extra close to the Earth. They are also 'blue Moons' as there are two of these in one month, on 2 and 31 January.

Chinese New Year falls in the middle of February and is, as always, set by the New Moon prior to the quarter-day 'Imbolc'. It's a time to clear out clutter, pay off debts and, if you can, enjoy the spectacle of the red dragon in your nearest Chinatown!

Pagans begin February with the fire-festival of Imbolc, the feast of the Celtic goddess Brid, which signifies the promise or the first glimpse of spring, when the first snowdrops appear. Ewes start to lactate and will soon give birth to the spring lambs. Farmers should then 'beat the bounds' of their land. This synchronises with the US festival of Groundhog Day, and with Candlemas, the Christian version of Imbolc, the end of winter. Many of the pagan festivals were absorbed into the Christian traditions, leading to a melding of pagan and Christian significance. So many rustic proverbs relate to this day, for example, from Germany, 'The badger peeps out of his hole on Candlemas Day/And if he finds snow, walks abroad/But if he sees the sun shining/Draws back into his hole'. In America there are similar traditions relating to groundhogs. Later in February comes *Mardi Gras*, which is Shrove Tuesday in the Christian calendar, just prior to a New Moon (that experiences a solar eclipse). A New Moon is a proper time for beginnings.

The Persian New Year is fixed on to the spring equinox 20 March. A few days earlier in the usual seasonal calendar is the festival of St Patrick's Day although, of course, this calendar is mostly focused on the lunar-defined events which make up the ancient sacred calendars of humanity. The Hindu New Year also comes around this time, at the New Moon of March, just prior to the equinox.

Christian Holy Week comes around the Full Moon at the end of March. Then, a month later, May Day and Beltane are the great life-affirming fire-festivals, to honour the fertility of spring. At Beltane, farm animals begin lactating, and sheep and cattle are put out to summer pastures. One should be up to greet the dawn and early-morning mists – after an all-night party, if you can! The traditional marking of May Day on 1 May is defined by our modern solar-month calendar, which did not exist when these ancient festivals marked out the eightfold turning of the year. We suggest that the old pagan festival of Beltane should be celebrated around 5 May, midway between the solstice and the equinox. See if your community can manage a May Queen and a maypole. The Buddhist festival of Wesak (the Buddha's birthday) happens on the Full Moon at the end of May.

The Islamic fast-month of Ramadan starts with the New Moon in mid-May, when Muslims are not allowed to eat *or drink* while the Sun is above the horizon, all through the heat of May–June. It is interesting to note that Islam was founded in a southerly latitude where the hours of fasting were shorter. That holy month is, or should be, experiential not calculated, starting when the first sliver of the New Moon is seen, which our calendar puts on the second day after the calculated New Moon.

Enjoy a glass of wine with friends on the June solstice (it's exactly at 11 am on 21 June): Earth and Sun are then mysteriously aligned with the galaxy on that longest day, as the Sun crosses over the Galactic Equator. To make sure the seasons are still turning properly, check out a St John's Wort plant – it should open up on St John's Day, 24 June. Naturopathic doctors still use this midsummer flower to treat 'moderate to mild' depression. This day is three days after the solstice for the same reason that Christmas is three days after the winter solstice, namely that (so we are told) this is when the Sun starts to move again – it 'stands still' on the solstice, that is what the word means. Let's try to experience again these once-vital setting and rising points on the horizon.

July begins with Aphelion, when Earth is furthest away from the Sun in its yearly course. We feel a paradox here, getting the most heat of the summer when furthest away from the Sun. Enjoy an outdoor summer barbecue around the Full Moon of 26 July, seeing the Full Moon rising as the Sun sets, and also an eclipse.

August brings the summertime holiday festival of Lammas, a 'gathering of the tribes'. The word Lammas alludes to the loaf made from the first new wheat, and so this summer's-end festival means the start of the harvest, a time of holiday, and the end of the crop-circle season. On 12 August watch the meteor shower after midnight.

The autumn equinox tips us into the dark half of the year, when Demeter, the Earth or corn-goddess, loses her lovely daughter, Persephone, who will reappear six months later. Soon after that comes the Harvest Moon, and then the Michaelmas festival comes a few days later.

In early October enjoy the Hunter's Moon rising, in the 'season of mists and mellow fruitfulness'. The Sun is passing through the sidereal sign of the Balance over this period, until 17 October – that's the same zodiac system used in this

Calendar for the Moon. The autumn this year sees Venus as the bright Evening Star rising highest in the sky after sunset in August. The Greeks called her *Hesperus*. She grows brightest in September, finally vanishing into the sunset in mid-October, and during this period of her marvellous celestial ballet she comes nearest to the Sun. Then, early-risers will see her in November as the Morning Star, 'Lucifer' growing most brilliant by the end of that month.

Samhain (pronounced 'sawain') on 7 November, marks the Celtic New Year and was the last chance for the clans to meet before winter. Our modern equivalents are Hallowe'en – mischief night! – and Bonfire Night. Nature dies back for another year, bringing an other-worldly flavour to this time of supernatural interference in human affairs: ghosts, ghouls and divination.

Sacred Moons of 2018

In our multi-cultural society it makes sense to honour the Sacred Moons of different cultures. The calendars of several of the great religions are founded on the lunar cycle and lunar-based sacred calendars still exist around the world. Many cultures begin their year on a New Moon, which is the proper time for new beginnings. The calendar gives these dates for five different world religions: Islam, Judaism, Christianity, Buddhism and Hinduism, as well as the Chinese State calendar. Let's make the honouring of these Sacred Moons of different cultures a socially cohesive force in the modern world.

Through these sacred events one can experience the concept of the dark time of New Moon as a beginning. In today's electric-light society one is hardly able to sense the significance of this time of the month when the Moon cannot be seen by day or night. Mental health, balance in life and happiness are all assisted by living more in tune with the lunar calendar.

Here are the 'Sacred Moons' of 2018, i.e. the Full Moons of Easter and Wesak (Buddhist) plus other New Moon festivals.

Chinese New Year	16 February,	New Moon on 16 February
	Year of the Earth Dog	
Hindu New Year	18 March	New Moon on 17 March
Easter Sunday	1 April	Full Moon on 31 March
Buddhist Wesak	29 May	Full Moon on 29 May
Start of Ramadan	16 May	New Moon on 15 May
Jewish New Year	10 September	New Moon on 9 September
Muslim New Year	12 September	New Moon on 9 September
Hindu Diwali	7 November	New Moon on 7 November

Further Reading

Barger, Adèle, *Gardening Success with Lunar Aspects,* American Federation of Astrologers, 1977.

Biodynamics: *New Directions for Farming and Gardening in New Zealand,* Random Century, N.Z., 1989.

Burns, J.T., *Cosmic Influences on Humans, Animals and Plants, An Annotated Bibliography,* Magill (US), 1997.

Culpeper, N., *Culpeper's Complete Herbal,* Foulsham, London.

Dariotus Redivivus, or a brief introduction to the judgement of the stars, 1653 (agricultural section by Nathaniel Spark).

Domin, A., Ed., *Organic Wholefoods, Naturally Delicious Cuisine,* Konemann, 1997.

Elliott, Jean, *Plants and Planets, Astrological Gardening,* self-published, 1996.

Estienne, C. & Liebault, J., *La Maison Rustique,* trans. Surfleet, 1616.

Gauquelin, Michel, *The Cosmic Clocks,* Pan Books, 1969.

Hill, T., *The Gardener's Labyrinth,* 1577, OUP, 1987.

Joly, N., *Le Vin du Ciel à la Terre,* Paris, 1997.

Kolisko, L., *Agriculture of Tomorrow,* Kolisko Archive Publications, Bournemouth, 1939, 1982.

Kollerstrom, N., *Farmers' Moon,* New Alchemy Press, 2014.

Kollerstrom, N. & Power, C., 'The influence of the lunar cycle on fertility on two thoroughbred studfarms', *Equine Fertility Journal,* 2000, 32, 75–77.

Kollerstrom, N. & Staudenmaier, G., 'Evidence for Lunar-Sidereal Rhythms in Crop Yield: A Review', *Biological Agriculture and Horticulture 2001,* 19, 247–259.

Lieber, A. L., *The Lunar Effect,* Corgi, 1979.

Playfair, G. & Hill, S., *The Cycles of Heaven,* Pan Books, 1979.

Pliny, *History of Nature,* Vol. 18, Section 75 (Loeb Classics, 1961).

Podolinsky, A., *Bio-Dynamic Agriculture Introductory Lectures,* Vol.1, Australia, 1990.

Powell, R. & Treadgold, P., *The Sidereal Zodiac,* Anthroposophical Publications, US, 1979.

Sattler, F. & Wistinghausen, E., *Bio-Dynamic Farming Practice,* CUP, 1989.

Shaw, Beth, 'Landmarks of the year', *Astrological Journal,* April 1997, 26–35. (Invaluable advice on seasons and festivals.)

Taylor, Peter, Chill, A Reassessment of Global Warming Theory, Clairview Books, 2009.

Temple, J., *Gardening Without Chemicals,* 1986.

Thun, M., *Gardening for Life,* Hawthorne Press, 2000.

Thun, M., *Results from the Biodynamic Sowing and Planting Calendar,* Floris Books, 2003.

Thun, M. and M., *When Wine Tastes Best,* Floris Books, 2009.

Index

Page numbers in **bold** indicate major references

animal husbandry 37, 45
annuals 62
apogee-perigee cycle **15–16**, 32, 62
April 50, calendar pages
aspects **40–43**, 60, 61
    Moon–Saturn 40, 41, 60
    Moon–Sun 60
    Moon–Venus 60
    solar 42–43
August 52–53, calendar pages

bio-dynamics 6, 18, 22
biosphere 8–9
Buddhist Wesak 139, 141

Chinese New Year 139, 140–41
crop production
    and the Moon 25–26, 27–33
    and solar eclipse 43
    and the Sun 23–25
crop taste 31–32

December 55, calendar pages
drought
    and nutation cycle 25–26
    and solar rhythm 25

Easter Sunday 139, 141
eclipses 16–17, 43
ecliptic plane 16–17
elements 61
    associated crops 56–57
    element-cycle **10–13**, 20, **27–31**

famine see drought
farming
    organic 5, 44–46
    traditional lore 9–10
    see also animal husbandry; crops; plants
February 48, calendar pages
fertility and Moon phases 34–39
festivals
    religious 6, 139, 141
    traditional 139–140

fish and fishing 39
Flower days 12
flowering plants 57, 60
folklore 9–10
four elements see elements
Fruit-seed days 13, 42
fruit-seed plants 57
Full Moon **14–15**, 32, **34–39**, 61
    festivals 139, 140–141

gardening
    organic 29, 45–46
    traditional lore 9–10
gelding **63**
geomagnetic field 8, 9
germination rate 34
global warming 26
grafting 59, 63

Harvest
    Moon 17–18
    timing of 38, **58–59**, 63
Hindu New Year 139, 140–41
horse breeding 37–38

January 47–48, calendar pages
July 52, calendar pages
June 51, calendar pages
Jupiter 42

Kew, a new year at 33

Leaf days 12
leaf plants 57
lunar calendar 64–138
    reading 60–63
lunar cycles 8, 10–13, **14–18**, **27–33**, **34–36**
    effects on biosphere 8–9
    element cycle 10–13
    festivals 6, 139–141
    lunar day 32–33, 59
    lunar month 12, 34–39
    nutation cycle 25–26
lunar eclipse 16–17

March 49, calendar pages
May 50–51, calendar pages

Moon
    aspects **40–43**, 60, 61
    and Earth 15–16
    and ecliptic plane 16–17
    Full Moon **14–15**, 32, **34–39**, 61
    Harvest Moon 17–18
    height in the sky 17
    influence on crop yields 25–26, 27–33
    influence on plants 5–6, 9–10, 12
    Moonrise 32–33, 59, 61, 63
    Moonset 59, 61, 63
    New Moon **14–15**, **34–39**, 61
    sacred moons 140–41
    and Saturn 40, **41**, 60
    and stars 15
    and Sun 14–15, 40
Moon cycles
    apogee-perigee **15–16**, 32, 62
    nodal **16–17**, 32
    sidereal 15, 27–32
    synodic (phase cycle) **14–15**, 32, **34–39**, 61
Moons of celebration 7, **140–41**
Muslim months 6, 139, 140–41

New Moon **14–15**, **34–39**, 61
nodal cycle 16–17, 32
nodes **16–17**, 32, 62
November 54–55, calendar pages
nutation cycle 25–26

October 54, calendar pages
organic movement 6, 45
    farming 44–45
    gardening 29, 45–46

perennials 60, 63
perigee **15–16**, 32, 62
Persian New Year 139
phase cycle (synodic) **14–15**, 32, **34–39**, 61
    and animal fertility 37–38
    and fish 39
    and harvest 38
    and plant growth 34–36
    and timber felling 38–39
planting, timing of 59
plants
    influence of Moon on 5–6, 9–10, 12
sensitivity to biosphere 8–9
    see also headings beginning with 'crop'
pruning 59, 63

rainfall
    and the lunar cycle 8–9, **25–26**
    and the solar rhythm 23–25

Root days 12, 28
root plants 57

Saturn 40, **41**, 60
September 53, calendar pages
sidereal cycle 15, 27
    and crop yield 27–32
sidereal zodiac 19–20, 22, 61
sky-triangles 11
Soil Association 45
solar eclipses 16–17, **43**
solar rhythm 23–25
sowing
    sidereal cycle 27–31
    timing of **27–33**, **58–59**, 63
star rhythm 11–13, 58–59
star zodiac **19–22**, 61
Steiner, Rudolf 5, 22, 36, 45
Sun and crop yield 23–25, 43
Sunspot cycle 23–25, 26
    and crop production 23–25, 43
    and rainfall 25
    and wine production 43
synodic cycle (phase) **14–15**, 32, **34–39**, 61
    and animal fertility 37–38
    and fish 39
    and harvest 38
    and plant growth 34–36
    and timber felling 38–39

Taylor, Peter 26
Temple, Jack 45–46
Thun, Maria **13**, 22, **27–28**, 32, **43**
timber felling 38–39
time zone adjustments 63
transplanting 63
trees 60, 63
trigons 11
trines 60
tropical zodiac 20–22

vegetable gardening
    monthly tasks 47–55
Venus **40**, 60
vine growing 42–43

wine tasting 18

zodiac
    four element cycle **10–12**, 20, **27–31**
    history 19–22
    sidereal zodiac 19–20, 22, 61
    star zodiac **19–22**, 61
    tropical zodiac 20–22